"$50K Webinar Blueprint." (TM)

This book is dedicated to all to aspire to take your webinar to the next level. The information provided by the marketers in this book will inform and motivate you for a lifetime.

Sammy, Shana, Nathan, Eric, Jake, JVZoo,

Special thanks to
My Why
Marie Heiland
Eric Rosenberg

Caveat Emptor

The materials in this book are from Online marketers who are making a difference in people lives doing webinars among other thingsLife changing for those who can learn from the best of the best.

TABLE OF CONTENTS

Introduction:

Hi everyone it's Rich Wilens.

I have been working with JVZoo and Webinarswaps since its inception. Working for JVZoo has given me the opportunity to host over 300 webinars on their platform. Not just one webinar from one vendor doing the same webinar over and over again, but over 300 webinars , with over 250 different products from over 250 different vendors.

I have seen the good, the bad, the ugly, the webinars that work and convert, the ones the tank and blank. Because of that experience, I have learned what works and what doesn't. Combine that with over 40 years sales experience, I have created a course to teach you how to properly prepare, produce promote, market and cash in with Webinars.

Webinars have always been one of the best tools to promote and sell your products. Whether you do it live or an evergreen recorded webinar, there is a proper way to do a webinar. Your webinar needs to have a strategic, formatted, and interactive way to get your attendees to say yes throughout the webinar giving you an opportunity to close more sales.

Thus, webinars and specifically webinar training is as important as your product.

The course is called $50K Webinar Blue print.. This course is designed to teach you how to take your product or service, and turn it into a properly structured webinar that will convert and increase your sales. You will learn how to do it live or recorded, gear it specifically to a niche or list or make it evergreen for maximum results.

This book and audio course is the first part of learning how to properly put together a closing webinar.

Now, who is this course for? This course is for everyone who has a product or service that wants to promote through webinars. This is for anyone who has purchased a webinar platforms such as Webinar Jam, EasyWebinar, Webinar jeo, Webinar Ignition, Webinar Income system and others.

This course is for anyone who use gotowebinar , ON24, Webex, Adobe connect, and global meet

These Webinar platforms all give their customers the interface and tools to present a webinar but usually teach the minimum on how to do a webinar. Most of these platforms teach how to do a webinar as a supplement for their platform and do not teach in depth strategies and techniques on how to do a Webinar properly.

I have complied years of research, education and experience to bring you the best, up to date training. I have done all the research. My sources include e. Brian Rose's How to make a killing with webinars, Lewis Howes Ultimate Webinar Marketing Guide, Sherri Rose's the webinar way, and other books and programs such as Webinar Master, Webinar Blueprint, Webinar Manifasto, Webinars made easy, etc, etc.

I have learned from all of these sources to bring you the best of the best.

The ease of learning from $50K webinar blueprint combined with the best up to date material is reason enough to get this product. It is perfect for your Internet marketing library.

Now, Why would you get this product from me? I'll share that with you. I have learned from the best marketers in the world, I have over 40 years' experience as a salesperson and closer, I work for one of the largest Affiliate marketing platform in the world and I have hosted over 300 webinars, and I am very well connected with all the top marketers. I'm the guy.....I'm your guy

Here's the Bottom line. You will learn how to produce, promote, market and most important convert and close and get more sales using a properly produced webinar.

This training course is a must for everyone who would like to promote their product through a live or recorded webinar. Whether your webinar is two minutes, 15, 30, 60 minutes or over two hours, you will learn how to maximize conversions with each presentation

You will learn tips and techniques how to create , market and polish up an existing webinar or just get you started and prepare you for our $50K webinar blueprint course.

I have seen the good, the bad, the ugly and the webinars that sold over 50K in sales. I have alone witnessed the ones who blanked. I have seen it all.

Since starting with webinarswaps, the webinar business has changed. No longer do you have just gotowebinar as the main platform to do webinars. Different webinar platforms have popped up and offer a variety of choices of platforms.

The content in this book is probable the most informative information you'll read on webinars. These marketers really know their stuff. When I decided to create this program I knew I was going to turn the audios into a book. It is hard to read this book interview style and yet you understand it and follow it along with the interview.

What I found the hardest thing to do was to find the separation of paragraph's and insert the punctuation. I did a terrible job and yet when I thought about the content I forgave myself. With that being said, you can follow along if you get the audio series and read the book as if the person was chatting with you.

To listen to the audios, check out the audio program at www.richwilens,com/programs.

Enjoy the information in this book.

Why this book can change the way you do webinars:

As I did these interviews with these Internet marketers, I realized I didn't know everything. With my experience doing webinars, I thought I learned a lot by participating in over 400 webinars while I was working for Jay the zoo.

I did so many webinars, I saw the good, the bad, the absolute worst closing ratios and the absolute best.

I thought I pretty much knew how to do a webinar.

It turns out, that you never stop learning. Especially in the Internet marketing field. The best way to make more sales, make more money, and concentrate on getting the information and your product out to a concentrated amount of people is the way of the future.

These are called webinars. Some people call them teleconferences, web classes, info commercials for the net, etc. etc.

What you will learn in this book, are the tips and tricks that will change the way you do webinars.

I've always believed that a webinar should be structured. Webinars can go anywhere from 45 minutes all the way up to three hours. 3 Hours Is Way too long to do a webinar and yet you will listen to some of the Internet marketers in this book that will say, three hours is not too long as long as there's one more person out there ready to buy.

You will learn different techniques, different ways to set up landing pages, thank you pages, registration pages, and how to structure your webinar.

This book is very unique because I participate in each one of the interviews giving my tips, tricks, and insights on how to do a proper webinar.

This book goes along with my product, 50 K webinar blueprint. 50 K webinar blueprint is a series of 12 modules that teaches you how to produce, promote, host, properly structure a webinar, how to close, went to close, the certain questions you need to answer and finally went to and your webinar. You can get this program on JVZoo.com or you can get it on my website www.RichWillens.com.

I suggest to you to read this book in its entirety. It might be a little choppy but I promise you you will get the information you need to see that the way you're doing webinars can be greatly improved.

Enjoy this book.

Daniel Hall

Today's guest is Daniel Hall. He is an attorney, he is also a registered nurse, an he fits right into the project I'm doing, this part of the 50k webinar blueprint. He is one of the original people who not only came up with the concept of doing webinars but the concept of doing webinars right. Please welcome to the program today Daniel Hall. Hello Daniel, how are you?

Daniel: I'm very good Rich, thanks for having me.

Rich: Well, it's absolutely my privilege. I remember years ago when I first started working with JVZoo and Webinarswaps you were one of the first people that we held a webinar with and I was amazed and fascinated at how organized and the things that you do to not only make webinars successful but you were kind of like one of the pioneers in the webinar industry.

I want to know when did you start with webinars and tell me a little bit of how you started it in the beginning anf how you progressed to where you are today.

Daniel: Well I'll tell you what, when I gave up practicing law in 2004 to basically do real estate investing and I was listening to a lot of the "real estate gurus" and they would sell these multi-thousand dollar packages or $10,000 packages and they were doing it via GoTowebinar, I would get on these things and I would listen to them and I'm like this is really cool and I sense that there was something there because at the time that was sort of the only niche that was really using webinars in the way that we use them today, no one was; no one that I knew anyway was actually doing it in the internet marketing space or the publishing area which where I attempted to focus, and so I'm thinking to myself, wow this is a very cool thing, i realized that the very best place to sell is from the platform, at a live event sort of eyeball to eyeball with your audience, I saw this platform as a very close second to that live interaction, that live event that you would present at; that being the webinars.

So I thought I need to figure out how to do this and I was very fortunate because a very good friend of mine- because I'm particularly tech savvy, I'm more of a sales guy that I am a tech guy.

So fortunately I was able to get some private tutoring learning the mechanics of setting it up with my friend Mike Stewart, and Mike sat me down on his couch and basically said ok, this how you set up a webinar; a GoTowebinar, you do this, you click here, you do this, and basically he walked me through the first webinar that I did, and when I first launched it, I don't know the exact date that I did my first webinar but it was probably 2008/2009, so it's been a while.

I remember doing the first one Rich, like for the first 3 months I tried these webinars and they were almost always promotional types and I would get to the pitch, do the pitch and I would essentially hear nothing, it was like cricket's tripping, no sales, no nothing. I'm just really glad I kept at it because I did finally figure out how to sell on a webinar, how to make a compelling webinar but also sell from it.

Basically the way that I do this is we always give massive value in the content portion of the webinar and I always want to make my guest feels as though, even if they don't take me up on my offer that they are getting value from the time that they are investing with me, and that ha served me very well over the years, just sort of that philosophy is let me provide value first, earn the right to make an offer and then make an offer, make a compelling damn good offer.

So that's sort of it in a nutshell.

Rich: Well let's take this from the beginning; we start with how you promote a webinar. Now, is there are a particular email sequence or any kind of way that you do, whether it's buying a Facebook ad, using somebody else's list or joint venturing.

When you go ahead and you want to put meat in the seat so to speak, fill it up, what kind of email sequence do you do in other to ensure a maximum amount of people not only opt in into your webinar but your show-up rate as well?

Daniel: Well it all begins with the topic you choose to present, I mean that's why people are coming, you need to have a sort of message to market match. In other words, if you're in the self-publishing niche which is where I am, things like SEO webinars don't do so well because it's not a message to market match for my community.

So that's the very first thing is make sure that whatever community you have or whatever community you're building that the message is right, that there is going to be some interest there, and I don't mean everyone on your list essentially needs to be tuned into it but a percentage, and this is art, it's some objective data that you see week to week and it's feedback as well from the people that you get.

 So that's the very first thing, you've got have a great message, a great hook as it were for a webinar. The second thing I do is I do a weekly webinar, so that's pretty important, either I'm doing it myself to my own list or I'm bringing in a joint venture partner to present to my list, and I do them generally on Wednesday morning or Wednesday early afternoon, and then I'll also do an encore of that same webinar the next day.

So typically what we will do is, let's say we're doing a Wednesday webinar, I will end the promotion from the previous week on a Sunday night and then start mailing for that Wednesday webinar Monday.

Rich: Two days before.

Daniel: Two days before. So we'll mail Monday, we'll mail Tuesday and we'll mail Wednesday in the morning if it's an early afternoon webinar, then we'll do the webinar.

If the webinar did well and there's obviously lots of interest I will typically then run an encore the next day and basically what an encore is is sort of a hybrid webinar where you use GoTowebinar to broadcast the previous day's video and you're also there or somebody on your team is also there live in the chat answering questions as well, and the reason why we do that is because it essentially will take what is usually a fairly dead day sale's wise and you'll see typically, if you had 50 sales on the night before or the afternoon before, the next day you'll see anywhere between 30 and 40 percent of the sales you saw on the first day, that's what I've seen, but I will not mail on a replay until the end of the encore.

So in that sort of sequence we'll do again Wednesday afternoon, probably Thursday evening; 6 O'clock or so and then I will start mailing the replay on Friday and again depending on when we end the promo we will generally send a pdf of some kind on Saturday.

So I typically will take the webinars and we'll have summaries prepared for them because that's a huge thing from a mailing standpoint, you're going to get much better opens and click through rates with the simple addition of the three letters pdf in your subject line on a Saturday, and if we're ending on a Sunday then we'll just role in to hey this is a last day kind of thing and we might even if it's doing really well, we might even mail to the unopened like 4 or 5 hours before the deadline. So that's the sequence Rich.

Rich: So let me just go ahead and recap. You mail out twice two days prior, you mail once on Monday, once on Tuesday, your webinar is on Wednesday. How many times do you mail on Wednesday for either your 3 O'clock or your 8 O'clock presentation?

Daniel: I'll mail usually once if it's early in the day or twice if it's later in the day'

Rich: Do you ever mail "we're starting now or live or 45 minutes," just to kind of prepare people that you're webinar is starting. I know you have a webinar trick that you use with GoTowebinar, can you share a little bit about that?

Daniel: Sure. To answer your first question, I don't send any external emails from my system or from my list basically saying starting now or starting in 30 minutes.

However, I do use the ability to change the title of a webinar in GoTowebinar which is what I'll do. So right before, let's say 30 minutes before I'll go in and change the title from whatever the title of the webinar is to brackets or parenthetical starting in 20 minutes and then send that out, and then GoTowebinar actually sends that email out and then usually right before I go live I'll say we're starting now, rename the title of the webinar and there is a little radio button in GoTowebinar that allows you to notify all participants that have registered and then we'll send out another email or another notice through GoTowebinar saying starting now usually.

Then the reason why I do that is I don't want to burn my list, I just want to mail to those people that raised their hand, that said I want to be on this presentation and this is something I'm interested in, so I just mail to that group.

Rich: And you know I was just talking about show-up rates a little bit earlier on my work and it's very important to increase your show-up rates and by having GoTo which is a feature they use and it's a hack that you can use in other to remind people that hey, we're starting now, and I'm assuming you do it just a couple of minutes before you hit the start button on that GoTo,

Not only does it save a spam complaint that you're mailing them too much but GoTo webinar is the one sending it out, and I think that's an absolute fantastic hack. How many do you think you can add from that, maybe another 10 or 20 people just from that mailing alone?

Daniel: It depends on what the registration rate was of course, this is a number's game as you know Rich, but I definitely see a difference if I don't go through that procedure, and in fact it's funny you should mention that, I often will get just compliments, "hey thank you for reminding me, I forgot this was going on now but thanks for letting me know." I'll actually get those compliments, I've never gotten a complaint that oh you're mailing me too much.

I'm talking about those folks that have raised their hands and said that they want to be on this live presentation. Which is another thing that I've done is when I'm personally doing a new product launch; I've tried to train my folks to be there live for a webinar because that's another big conversion booster.

The more people that you have live on the webinar the better your conversions are going to be versus those people that are going to wait around and essentially watch on their time. So one of the things I've tried to train my people to do is to show up- when they know it's going to be another real fast product that we're launching is to absolutely change their schedule, make sure that they are there live, if they have to get a babysitter, I don't care what they have to do, just be there live for my live events when I'm launching a new product because I always give some sort of incentive to those folks that are there live versus those folks that will listen later on a replay.

So they've come to know me over years of me just doing that, and I'll even insinuate in my emails, "hey, if you can, be there live. You definitely don't want to miss what I have for you," you know that sort of thing and then follow up on it as well. So that's sort of on a side but another little hack that is again a conversion boaster.

Rich: Well let's just go ahead and recap real quick and then we're going to move on. You send out an email a day, one if you're having the webinar on Wednesday, two days prior you'll send out one on Monday, one on Tuesday, you'll usually send out an early morning mail on the day of the webinar.

You don't necessarily go ahead and say we're starting in one hour or we've already started come on, and one of the ticks and hacks that you use is GoTowebinar gives you the option to change your webinar title and notify other participants. So it sounds like it's four good tips when it comes to promoting these webinars and putting people in the seats. Let's talk about the introduction, how long do you think an introduction should be and what is it do you think that you'd like to introduce then?

Daniel: Alright, so the intro is relatively important, the intro only needs to be enough to let folks know you know what the heck you're talking about and that's it.

I mean, they don't want to know about you or your accomplishments or anything like that, they just want to know you know your stuff well enough for them to stick around, that's it.

Rich: I notice when you do your intros and a lot of your webinars you always do a caveat and it seems like you make a promise in the beginning of the webinar and I believe you make this promise that if I deliver this program as sponsored and at the end of this I'm asking your permission to go ahead and present whatever it is that you're going to present at the end. Can you elaborate a little bit on how you start that webinar and make that promise?

Daniel: I think a lot of business and long term business is having the integrity that you're going to sell, so very I'm unapologetic about the fact that I'm about to sell you something and I'm going to give you really good value, even if you don't buy you definitely want to stick around, but I want to let you know before we go very far here that there is going to be an offer.

So I always start all of my broadcast with that sort of hey this presentation is sponsored by whatever the product is and we will have a way for you to continue your education with us, so again you're going to hear an offer.

More or less is what I tell them, then I also go into the promise part of it, and I'll say something like but before I do, right?

Before you hear any more about this I'm going to deliver on my promise to you, and I'll say, "And you might be wondering what is that promise. So here it is", and I'll just go through and read whatever I'm tending on presenting on that presentation, and then also right after the promise I'll say, "hey, is this why you showed up, is this why you're here?" because engagement is also very important on a live webinar, so I'll start getting yeses very early on, because again this goes back to Robert Cialdini, people want to be consistent with the decisions they've made in the past.

So if you get people starting to say yes early on and frequently all the way through its statistically easier for them to day yes to your offer when you ask them for the sale.

So I'm also setting that up during that time as well, and I'm also setting up sort of the quid pro quo. In some of my presentations I'll even throw in and say something like listen, now you know my promise, what I'm about to say is going to seem counter intuitive to you, you're going to hear it and you're going to say, wow are you really saying this, and I just want to assure you I'm really saying this and I really do mean this, and I say at the end of the presentation as I said earlier we're going to be having an offer for you but I don't want you to invest in it, I don't want you to invest in it unless I make good on my promise to do so, and if I do deliver on my promise then you should feel obligated to take advantage of our special offer at the end of the presentation if and only if it's right for you.

Does that sound fair?

Go to your questions box and say fair. And again you're getting agreement and commitment early on in the webinar process. So that's another thing that we do, and again I don't chain people to their computer, if they don't like what's going on, leave! I don't profess to being right for everyone so I don't try to please everyone which is another thing.

This is the way I run my business and either it matches with how you like things done or it doesn't. So this is how I do my business, and most people seem to just appreciate the forthrightness of it and we go forward.

Rich: And you know what? It's very good because you had you shaking your head yes, and it's an old sales technique if you can just go ahead and continue shaking your head yes and people start shaking their head yes, you wind up having your attendees agree with you, and even though you're not doing this on a one to one; on a personal level where they can see you, you are doing it on a one to one regardless of how many people are on the webinar, because most people don't know there's 500 or a thousand people on the webinar or there is 50 or 200.

One of the techniques that I use is I talk to one individual on the program and whether it's somebody I know who's been there before, who you even necessarily know will not buy but you know they ask you the smart questions, I think this is very important as well.

So in recapping, you go ahead and you make sure your customer start to engage. Now there is a question box and a chat box in GoTo webinar, do you have a support staff or somebody who works that backend and how successful are you in converting those people on the backend, whether it's converting them that night or in a follow-up?

Daniel: So the answer is yes, on every big webinar we work the chat. The chat is really important and so underused by most webinar presenters and in fact I can do better with it, but the fact is the more engagement you have in a webinar the better your bottom line is going to be, the better it's going to be for your sales., and basically it's because people are invested, they are actually taking the time to interact with you, to engage with you and the more of that engagement, the more of that interaction.

Again it goes back to the whole consistency, they want to be consistent with oh I've spent my valuable time which by the way is the only commodity that none of us get back, I mean we could all make more money but we can't make more time, when we take that dirt nap that's it, right?

Rich: You cash in those chips and- you know I have a saying, it's better to have halitosis than no breathe at all. There is a short time on this earth and if you're going to spend a time specifically on a webinar you want to make it worth it, and engagement is very important, sometimes people will type in the number one, you want to get them to engage but you also want to make it a little easier as well.

One of the techniques I use is I have them type in a one or type in a yes and get them to get used to doing that because it's all part of the engagement.

Now, on the backend in the question box you are correct, most people underutilize the benefits of having the chat box and the question box.

One technique I like to use is getting phone numbers. Have you ever tried to get phone numbers on the backend where even if they don't buy you can at least have a phone number where you can give them a call, have a personal engagement and then try to close them on the product?

Daniel: The price points of my product don't really lend themselves well to taking up time like that because essentially we have very affordable price points, our price points go from basically $97 to about $500.

So for a lot of these types of transactions they're impulse but that's an excellent tip especially for a higher ticket items on webinars. Then the other thing that I just wanted to circle back around and my friend John S. Rhodes does this really well is he'll use the chat box and he'll be listening to the webinar if somebody is presenting the webinar and he will take bits and basically write little tweets about what people just heard and the significance of what they just heard and type that back out in the chat and broadcast it back out to the chat to everyone watching.

Again, it's more social proof, it's thinking for people because remember are so overwhelmed, right? To the extent you possibly can't - and this goes back to the presentation, you have got to connect the dots, it's not enough for you to basically put the dots on the page and then say go from one to two, no you've got to draw the picture, you have got to do the work, you have got to do the thinking for your audience, leave as little as possible to their inference, right?

Super important, that's so important. So this idea of engagement and letting folks know, did you just hear what the presenter said?

So that's a very cool technique that again I see not very many people do it and those that I do see actually use that technique do very well.

Rich: And you know especially if increases one or two sales we always say it's the little things that you want to do and if can increase just one sale or two sales, well depending on what your average price point is, split in half with an affiliate, that's two times more money that you're going to be able to throw into your gross profit.

Do you have people working the backend? I know you are a presenter and as a presenter you're concentrating on the PowerPoint, you have a structured presentation, you know what you have to say next, you are anticipating objections, you really can't do it all at once.

Now some people are able to do that, read the question box and read the chat box, I think it takes away from the presentation. How do you handle that, do you have a support person that handles the backend or do you handle it yourself?

Daniel: I do. Oh no, I can barely walk and chew gum and I certainly can't be presenting and typing. I use the Columbus method of typing even till this day, it's like you hunt and you land, so you definitely don't want me on the chat. It's like…

Rich: Exactly, that's just being old school, I understand that. You know it is important not only to work the backend. We've talked about the intro at the beginning of the webinar, we know that you have somebody that's going to be working the backend and just basically firing up, participating not only with the attendees who have questions but getting the people to participate with you.

What about this story? The hero's journey I call it, it's about me. I was on a webinar just a couple of weeks ago where the hero's journey took 23 minutes before he actually got into his content.

What do you think about the hero's journey, what do you think about the hero's journey, what is it you think about yourself and how long do you keep your hero's journey or the about me before you go into content?

Daniel: I keep it exceedingly short. One of the things that I am known for is consistently excellent content. If the presentation calls for it fine, if it's more of an inspirational type of thing or if it's a mindset kind of thing then I can see where that might work out well or better, but from what I do I'm just like right into the content, we don't spend time yacking about whatever, that's not we do.

I'm not saying that it doesn't work; it's just not my approach.

Rich: Well I like to keep, if you're going to do an intro, an about me, people don't really- and again this goes back to old school selling technique.

People don't care how much you know until they know how much you care, and I think anybody can go ahead, let's say go to a car dealership, take a test drive in a Ferrari, drive to the coast where I live here in Naples, park in front of a mansion and just throw your phone to the salesman and go, "hey why don't you take a picture?" and the next thing you know you're putting that on your sales page or your about page, and you know that just doesn't cut it, everything is credibility.

So I like to keep it around a minute and half or two minutes, just like you said if there is a story, an important story that your attendees are engaging I think that can be but never longer than 3 or 4 minutes because people aren't there to hear about you, they're there to learn.

Daniel: Just so we're very clear about this, where you can use case studies from people like your audience, because they may not relate to you like you're this person, you're the authority, you're the guru, you're the leader, of course you can do this stuff, what about me?

I don't have this, I don't have that, I don't have this ability, I shrink if I have to get up and talk before an audience or whatever the thing is. If you're going to use stories and we do this, this is what we do because it makes it easier to relate the content to them, right?

We'll use case studies of people like them that illustrate some point or some concept that we have put forward. So that I think is super important and it's sort of a more believable hero's journey because it's one of them.

Rich: Right and you know what? It's kind of unrealistic to assume that the people on your webinar is going to buy a $199 product have an airplane, like in a mansion and drive a Ferrari. So they're there for one reason and that is to better themselves and even though you might have those things whether they're true or not, why throw it into somebody's face?

I think there is a right way and a wrong way to do that, and I think coming across as being better off than your audience and basically bragging about it doesn't really give that rapport and build that relationship that you want to build with somebody that you're going to be asking for a $199 later in the program.

So you not agree?

Daniel: Yeah, by in large I agree with that.

Rich: Good. I know you've got your own products, do you ever do affiliates, do you ever mail to your own list, let's say I come to you for example and say Daniel I've got a program, I call it a webinar on webinars and I would like to present it to your list.

Do you ever joint venture with other people and how well do you do and do you take in consideration what's going to be good for your list or do you just pretty much throw anything up there just to try to generate some additional revenue on a webinar?

Daniel: So the most important asset if you're in this game for a long term and I am is basically tending to your flock as it were.

I often say that I'm the mother hen and my community are my chicks, and it's ny job to raise them in whatever their endeavor is, get them through the farm yard without a chicken hawk attacking them and also teaching them what it takes to survive and thrive.

So that's sort of my approach to how I treat my community. So there are far fewer programs that I would put in front of my community than I get pitched for, I mean I get pitched weekly to do something or another that I just say no. it's pretty difficult, as a matter of fact to the second point on joint ventures, I typically- yes I do joint ventures, that's a pretty big part of my business actually, but the thing is I only choose probably one or two new joint venture partners a year because they need to be vetted, I've got be able to feel good about working with them and fortunately I have a pretty big stable people I trust, that have a track record, they treat my people the way I want them treated.

So once you sort of have this network established it's pretty easy to do a new training webinar every week with somebody. I think that answers your questions.

Rich: Well it does, and let me share- in fact I'm sure you remember this. I once approached you, I had a client, his name was Chip Cooper, Chip Cooper is an attorney, he's an adjunct professor I think at the university of North Carolina, he's got a boutique, law firm out of Atlanta and he got into the legal field for internet marketing where he was creating a program that had to do with creating documents like terms of service and privacy policy etc.

I remember approaching you and you being an attorney in the past said you know what, I've got to check this guy out. You did, wound up having a great webinar and I see that you use it in some of your webinar materials now. Is that what you mean by vetting the clients that you have because you have such a good rapport and respect for your list?

Daniel: Exactly. I've got to know that whoever I'm putting in front of people that they're going to treat them in the same way that I or substantially similar way that I would, and I'm not going to tell you that I am perfect, I'm far from perfect, but if somebody burns my folks or does something that I don't like they're out, I mean forever out, no second chances, that's it.

Rich: Of course you know your list is very important to you, you build the rapport and a relationship with your list so much so that when you do recommend something your list trusts you and if you're going to recommend somebody and you just bring in the wrong guy you lose a little bit of that trust and it costs you because your list is so important.

Daniel: Exactly.

Rich: So I know you've got your own products and you've got four different products, I believe we chatted about that a little bit earlier and I know you've done these products on webinar swaps when we were doing webinar swaps back in the day, content is very important to you.

Do you have a certain structure that you do on a webinar and I believe you were talking about 45 minutes of just pure content before you go into the Q&A or the sales pitch?

Daniel: it depends. I don't know, it's different for each presentation although I would say if you can get through your close in an hour which just means present and actually finish your pitch in an hour, then basically at the time frame start taking questions, that's a good goal.

Now I frequently miss the mark on that and I'm way over as you well know, but that's sort of what I am trying to do, and I realize in some of my presentations we bite off more than we can chew because I do like to give tons of great value, so I'll teach probably a little too long, but in the final analysis it's also about what value are you adding to the lives of folks in your audience. If you're truly adding value to their lives, making their lives better then it's going to benefit you long term.

Rich: And you know what? That's a very true statement, what you want to do is you want to deliver. You know the term "over deliver" is battered and is thrown around and it's pretty easy to say, however if you believe that you're over delivering, what is actually over delivering?

That's doing a 110%, there's no 110%, there's basically a 100%. You talked about trying to wrap things in an hour, I know sometimes you've gone on and held one webinar and before you even got to the close you were delivering an hour and half worth of content.

When you find people's attention span are usually 51 minutes, sometimes you do go over and go to that hour and hour and 15 minutes, what do you judge your clients? Do you judge on participation if you're going to go longer than that hour?

Daniel: I judge on the content that I am presenting, if it's really hardcore stuff. I remember some of my most successful webinars went on for hours.

I was probably one of the first guys to have a kindle webinar. We would teach people how to publish their books on kindle which is another little hack, and we would close and we would say listen, we're going to do for those folks that are buying right now, like right now, we're going to take 15 minute break, don't go anywhere because I'm going to tell you how to go to a bonus webinar that was pure content and it was something sexy.

Usually with that one we would do how to make your book amazon bestselling book, and it would be total time with the kindle webinar, the close, the Q&A and then the bonus webinar, I would be on for 4 and half hours with people.

Rich: And you find that people actually stay through that 4, 4 and half hours? They say that a person's attention span on a webinar is 51 minutes. How do you justify being on for 2, 3, 4 hours?

Daniel: I justify it by the money in my bank account.

Rich: I guess that's important too. If people are going to stay if they're interested in the content I imagine they're going to stay till the end, and that some people do you know we're going to give you a free bonus, so we're going to give you something and we're going to do this at the end of the webinar, so it entices them not only to stay, but sometimes those people are the ones, they're not necessarily your buyers, they just want something for nothing.

Daniel: Right.

Rich: So you've given your content, you've gone anywhere from 45 minutes to 2 hours depending on read that you get from your attendees, now it's time for the Q&A. Now, we all know what the objections are when it comes to our own product.

Do you know what the objections are, of what people won't buy and do you actually when you present these questions, do you present it like you're talking to an attendee or do you just go ahead and throw out those questions and then answer it to eliminate the objection?

Daniel: It's sort of in the moment, on how I'm feeling it's best going to land, right? So I'll do it either of those ways, depending.

Rich: Got you. You know I like to suggest to people and especially people who are hosting, or not hosting but having their own webinar and product that even though you can put a thousand people on the GoTowebinar, you can actually communicate with one person because that one person doesn't know if there's a thousand people on or not, you don't have the advantage of looking out into the seat of your audience and seeing a thousand people.

So when you're communicating on a webinar you're communicating on a one on one and talking to one person at a time but that one person that you're talking to or 1000 people feel like you're talking to them. Now, the questions that come in the question box most of the time we already know what those questions are, so what I suggest is that you prepare those objection questions in advance and you can say something like, "Daniel says the price is too high and let me go ahead and address that now" or "Michael says he needs to talk about it with his wife, he'll talk to his wife before he purchases it" and what you want to do is you want to overcome all the objections because that's where sales comes in, once you overcome all the objections, you eliminate all the objections you solve their problem people are more or likely ready to purchase now.

So during the Q&A, how long is your Q&A and when you wrap up your Q&A do you go right into your sales presentation, your sales pitch?

Daniel: I do the pitch before I do the Q&A, that's super important.

Rich: And you put your buy button out there first before you go into the Q&A?

Daniel: Absolutely.

Rich: Do you have an actual sales page, I notice you do a PowerPoint, do you have PowerPoint or do you send them to a sales page where they actually purchase it through either a link or do you go and give them a link while you're doing your webinar?

Daniel: So we give them the link while they're going around the webinar, so that's the thing. Here's the other thing you want the sale now, you want it ASAP, you don't want things to happen necessarily, for them to forget or whatever, they have a dental expense and now they can't buy it, whatever it is.

You want the money in your bank account now, right? So I put the buy link out during that time and it seems to work pretty well.

Rich: Now, do you use scarcity when it comes time for people to buy, I know it's very important, once people leave it's more likely than not that they're aren't going to purchase it even if they get hold of the replay.

So there is an old adage, I'm here you're here the product is here, what is stopping us from doing business now? So the most important thing is to take advantage of it now.

What do you do, do you use scarcity to ensure that people have to make the decision now rather than wait for a replay or no decision at all?

Daniel: I often would say in one of my closes, hey listen, I realize that you may be on the fence and it's my job to knock you off that fence in one direction or the other and give you the information you need to make an informed decision, so if you have questions on this make sure you get it into the chat box let's address this now, maybe this isn't for you, maybe it is, we don't know yet.

So I'll basically seed the audience in that way and also I wanted to say that... going back to what you were saying about Chip and who by the way is a great guy, I think that if you're giving people value all the way through, and it's very apparent that you've given value all the way through, the ides is hey if this is what we're getting for free just imagine how good it's going to be when we actually pay this dude.

Rich: And here's another thing too, when you deliver your content and I believe you should always deliver your best content, do you deliver your best content?

Daniel: That's a subject of opinion, but yes I do. I will, it's very important that you sort of trod out your sexiest stuff and teach it and I think that's one of the things that's really important as well that if you effectively set up the pitch such that your audience actually sees themselves using the product, the system, whatever it is the more sales you're going to make which again sort of goes back to one of the reasons why if you can use case studies you want to use as many as those as possible because it's social proof, if you can tell the story of people that have used whatever it is that you're selling as you're teaching and implant that, that's also a very powerful strategy.

Rich: And you what? It's very important too, for all businesses it's very important, somebody may not buy from you that day but they might be on another webinar that you're presenting and they might buy from you as well, plus it's the referral part, everybody has got a friend and a friend of a friend.

So one referral begets another referral begets another attendee and out of those attendees depending on what your closing ratio is, that will determine if you're going to sell one more product or not.

Speaking of closing ratios, Daniel I know you're a presenter's guy and you're probably broken it down, and I know things are different with every webinar but what is basically a general closing percentage for you?

Daniel: It varies, it completely varies. Some of highest closing percentages have been in the low percentage points, high 20's consistently and that's about as good as I've ever done which is pretty damn good.

Let's face it, we've brought in hundreds of thousands of dollars doing that, but it depends, it depends on the price point, it's not uncommon to see pretty consistent 10, 12, 15 percent closing rate.

Rich: And you know you're a superstar, you're a baseball player, baseball player considered a superstar making millions of dollars, basically hits about 340 or 300 which tells me every ten times that he comes up to bat he strikes out or he gets an out seven times, so to hit on 3 out of ten.

Was talking a little bit earlier this morning about closing percentages and ratios, if your closing ration is 10 to let's say 15 percent, let's just take 10 percent, if you have a hundred people on and your closing rate is 10% that means you're going to sell 10 pieces.

So if your product is a 495 product, lets round it off to 500, you're basically making $250 times ten which is basically $2500 and that's based upon 100 attendees.

Does it upset you or does it bother you if somebody only brings in only 70 attendees to 100 attendees?

Daniel: No, absolutely not, those folks that are there are meant to be there, so that doesn't upset me at all. As a matter of fact, that's sort of my cut off, if I can joint venture with somebody that can put on at least 100 attendees chances are we're going to make some good money.

Rich: And that's very important. A lot of times I notice some presenters when they want to do a webinar with either webinar swaps or Rich Wilens webinar or JVZoo, like one big named guru says can you put 500 people on otherwise I don't want to do it.

I find that ridiculous because people who do show up to the webinar, who opt in, they're coming to see you and whether it's one person or 100 persons here's your opportunity to make a customer and a customer for life, and what's more important, to have a customer for life that bought from you once before because if they do buy from you more likely than not they would buy from you again, do you agree with that?

Daniel: I do absolutely agree with that. You've sort of touched on one of the big problems and we need to wrap up here soon but one of the big problems with webinars is getting people to actually- are there enough people that can actually put butts on seats, can actually put people on the webinars? And for the most part the answer is no, most folks even some of the big name gurus if you do joint partnership with them and you're thinking we're going to see all these great numbers, I've been disappointed countless times with what I'm like oh my gosh, my perception of what I thought you could do is quite a bit different from the reality.

So yeah, that's what I say if you get to a joint venture partner that can consistently put 100 people or more live on a webinar, that's good, you're doing good, and that's one of the things I'm always looking to do with all of my webinars is can we do 200, we did one yesterday, we were right at 200 live on the webinar which is these days damn good, ok?

Because there's another thing going on here and that's fatigue of the marketplace, not necessarily your audience but the marketplace in general with webinar options. So again goes back to so many hours in a day, and this another reasons why I take great pains to put out really freaking great webinar content so that people know, oh Daniel is doing it, I'm showing up, because there's so many choices out there, there's so many webinars people can go on and attend, they can only be on one of them one at a time, generally speaking.

Rich: So you've given us some awesome tips and if we wanted to get a hold of you Daniel, how would we be able to get a hold of you to find out not only about your products but if you're going to be having a webinar, what your schedule is, if we wanted to get a hold of you how would we do that?

Daniel: Well the best thing I would say to do is first and foremost jump on and subscribe to my podcast at realfastresults.com/itunes because I am- this a slightly different take and a really good thing about the podcast is that there's no offers being made, it's pure content.

You can kind of see what I like to cover and how I like to do things and by the way the real fast results podcast, each one of those is meant to be a is meant to be a free standing information product complete with all the steps, all the resources, everything that you need to actually get a result and get the promise delivered on that we've sort of put forth in the title of the podcast. So again, realfastresults.com/itunes, then my hub is at danielhallpresents.com.

Rich: And most of your products are called real fast this and real fast that, I know you're thinking about 4 of them, can you tell me what those are real quick before we go?

Daniel: Actually I've got 23 real fast products.

Rich: Ok, we don't have time for 23, but if you want to know about real fast products just go ahead on danielhubspresents.com and you'll be able to get all the information you need. Daniel thank you so very much for participating in my 50k webinar blueprint, you were beyond expectations as always I appreciate and I thank you very much.

Josh Zamora

RICH: And hello everybody and welcome to another edition of 50k webinar blueprint, my name is Rich   Wilens. Thank you so much to joining us today. It's a generous day, we're broadcasting live from   the Gulf of Mexico on west coast in Florida and my new home town of Naples. With me today is   a very special guest who's on the other side he is in the east coaster in the great state of Florida, Please say Hi to my friend Joshua Zamora, Hi Josh! How you doing?

JOSH: Great, Great to be here and yeah I'm on the South East Coaster…

RICH: I like that south east coast. Hope you like going by Joshua or by Josh because I could be flexible   either what you can…

JOSH: Josh is fine, my mom's one of the people that calls me Joshua!

RICH: Yeah! Okay you know I got you. My mother used to call me Richard especially every time I used   get in trouble, Richard! Richard... [Laughing] I knew i was in trouble when I did that. So this program is called *50k webinar blueprint* by putting it together in a program not only a program that's going to have these hangouts but I'm going to go ahead and not only print it up put it in the book, but there are also going to give away the audio and we are basically talking about how people can make $50,000 on a webinar.

Now, you been doing webinars for how many years now?

JOSH: For about 2 and half years now

RICH: Okay and when you doing webinars, do you do webinars with your own products or do you   basically do join ventures with other people who have their own products.

JOSH: Yeah, I've done the little bit of both. So, sometimes I do webinars just for my higher ticket   products,   sometimes   I   do webinar just to kind of warm my list up to lower ticket products.

So I do demo or my live software and it's kind of lead them into the sales page. I start the webinar   on 10 "o" clock and then once we got live at 11 boom! That's when I open up doors and push up my business sales page.

RICH: Now do you mostly do webinars for your list? Now when you're doing your own product, do you do mostly for your own list or do you also do it your webinar free to your product for other people's list?

JOSH: Yeah! I'll do both. So I do webinars to my own list, to my own products and then I will do webinar to my own list for other people's products. Now I do more of promoting other people's products. I've done some for my own webinars, but I'm still having doubt that I didn't do it completely so I do a little bit better when I promote other people's webinar.

RICH: Let's talk about doing other people's webinar. Do people approach you and they say I have got a great product. How do you determine if this product is going to be good for your list? And how do you determine if you really can actually bring to the table 100, 200, 500, to 1000 people?

JOSH: Yeah, absolutely I get message all the time from people who have a good webinar. I think my list might be a good fit so one thing I definitely look at of course is what makes the product is about the content on the webinar also plays a big role, and I know for me my list personally likes pretty much anything to do with video, SEO, SEO niche Sites, anything about ranking in Google, and also any unique traffic strategies as well, and also anything having to do with I have done two webinars around paid video traffic.

So YouTube ads and Facebook video ads, so things like that anything having with doing with the video I know it will do well for me.

RICH: Is that what you specialize in? You specialize in SEO and video?

JOSH: Yeah! Absolutely most of my products, most of my trainings I say probably 95% of it is all around   videos,   video ranking, video marketing and all around that.

RICH: Does video marketing works?

JOSH: Yeah, absolutely I mean I have been doing video since 2010. So it's something that's easy that anyone can do you knows there is camera on pretty much every device we have now.

So it's really no excuse to get off camera, I mean you can now look at Facebook live. I mean this video is just, I mean if you keep on doing video, I mean they are losing a lot of money out there.

RICH: You know it's funny that you mentioned that because I have started losing a lot of weight and because I tried to motivate myself. I take my phone with me and I started doing video live now.

The first time when I would go out, and I do some walking and I say people are going to walk with me so spend like an hour having people walk. I said to myself well that's pretty ridiculous nobody's going to want to spend an hour with me but you're absolutely correct with all of the phones, and everything we have all they have to do is hit Facebook live and bam! You are live and people who are actually following you or if you're on their Facebook feed and they click on and they go, they have interaction.

So I can see how video is very important and it certainly is the way of the future. So when somebody approaches you and they have product, is doing video or SEO or something that's going to fit your list.

What do you do in the beginning from the communication? Let's say for example Josh I've got a new video product, is coming out I'd like to do a webinar for your list, tell me how to go from there.

JOSH: Perfect, so the first thing that I look for is of course a webinar replay or somewhat of the recap of what the actual offer is. Because I like to see how first of the content that shared on the webinar I like to post webinars where there's at least some kind of good content or free content being given out that ties into the product. Those tend to convert really, really well from me.

Although, one time there was one that really kind of surprised me. It was a webinar where the young lady just pretty much jumped on some case studies, shared a little bit of what she is doing and then boom! Jumped right into the software and that went pretty well which was unexpected.

So sometimes you get those curve balls where you don't really need too much free content to be shared beforehand for it to do well.

I post the webinar and boom! she shared about 10 minutes of case studies and then jumped into the demo and boom on my list love the product, and it was really good products so sometimes you have those curves involved but for the most part I like seeing the webinar we played first to see what kind of content is shared, and then to get an idea of how the offers presented, what the offer is and see how that plays into what my list likes.

RICH: And it is very important that you know the structure of the webinar will fit not only with your list, but it will fit with the flow of webinar because let's face it, once you have a structured webinar you want to make sure that everything builds', builds' to that crescendo so when it comes time when you finish the question and answer or even before that you're ready to present the sales page, and I think that's an awesome story where you know some people just come in and they go.

Here is the testimonial, let me show what the product is and it just knocks out all the BS.

JOSH: Yes!

RICH: And want to do that would some webinar because you know there fluff on all the webinars, so you've got a product, you've done your wedding you see its going to be good fit for you. Now, it's time to put meet in the seats.

How do you put meet in the seats and you do it through an e-mails sequence? Do you do SEO? Do you buy Facebook ads? Do you do video ads? What is it that your specialty that puts bodies in the seats and you fill up is your attendees on the webinar?

JOSH: Yeah, absolutely not the first thing that I think is the most important is to be 100% committed to the webinar from the beginning. If you are not 100% committed from the beginning, then you're not going to put your entire effort to make sure that people are in the room because I think that's the biggest thing, you can get people in the room I mean you're going to have good webinar for the most part of this.

Assuming that everything else plays perfect and the offer is good, the content good, and everything matches at once you read all of that and you're 100% committed just go all out, that's what I do.

When I find a good webinar that I know it's going to be a good fit, and that's one of the reasons why I might see the webinar replays as well. So I can get an idea of what's being shared on the webinar and write my emails based around that content.

So I started hinting to that, this is what you're going to run once you join us on the webinar. So I used that as my kind of EMO to get them on the webinar. From the beginning, I just start emailing, I usually email 2 times a day leading up to the webinar usually like I have in the about 3 days to build up to the webinar, so the first day I email twice the second day I email twice, and the day we go live I email at least three to four times to ensure that people are getting on and also I try to make sure that I'm getting constant updates from the presenter of how many people I'm getting on the webinar and if those numbers are lacking then I push, I push harder. I want to make sure that I'm getting as many people as I can on online.

RICH: What kind of webinar platform do you use? Do you use GoTo webinar? Do you use webinar jam? Webinar Geo? Anything webinar recognition?

JOSH: For sales webinars right now, I still use GoTo webinar. To be honest, I just haven't experimented with any other platforms out there. I have also used webinars Jam quite a bit. Webinar jam I usually like to use that for just free content webinars or if sell a for a week book camp kind of thing I use webinar Jam for that just because I don't have to worry about selling anything. But in sales I like using go to webinar.

RICH: Got you, and you know it's very important that you pick the right platform. It seems that even though GoTo webinar is just that a little bit more expensive, thank God I don't know about you but you know it's still $87 a month from me, and I can have those on webinars but now I understand you really have to deliver on these webinars because to make it cost-effective, I understand GoTo webinar in order to have a thousand people on there as close to $500, and that's why all these other programs have come out like webinar Jam. How do you like using webinar Jam by the way?

JOSH: Yeah, I actually like webinar Jam it works perfectly with hangout. I never really had any issue, the only issue I ever had I did try using it for a sales one-on-one time, and the issue was totally on my part.

I wasn't too experienced with it at the time to be able to kind of run the way it supposed to run because the way it runs is you kind of preset your offer before you get on the webinar. So that once you ready to present your offer you just hit one button and the offer kind of pops out to all the customers and they can click on it and take advantage of the offer. So I kind of configure that all are wrong and when I want to go show the offer, it didn't work so It went to mess from that point but overall it's a really great platform I love how easy it is to get started. How I don't have to worry about our recording it because runs through YouTube and get automatically recorded and uploaded to my account and the interaction with the user, with the people on the webinar is very easy as well. It's just chat box, I think its works perfect.

RICH: You know I'm glad that you mentioned that it does get uploaded to YouTube. Do you use YouTube as a platform for your videos or do you have something like Vimeo or some other platform where you can present your video?

JOSH: No! I put everything on YouTube; I think they have the strongest platform. I mean even my sales videos; I put them on YouTube just because I never had an issue with them. They always upload superfast. I have tried using Vistia and Vimeo sometime and for me personally find that just take extra 2 seconds to load. So I'd rather just go with YouTube and have that blazing fast speed.

RICH: You know it's funny but GoTo has improved their recording in the replay. So once that you hit the record button and GoTo, it records it and once you end and you stop recording. Its start to ask you, Do you want to format this into an MP4 which you click on yes, and then you go back to GoTo and its say upload your recording. So not only does it convert but you can go ahead and upload you're recording to GoTo, and I never really had a problem with that. However, I do like using YouTube as well so depending on how you're going to SEO and get people to see your YouTube video of course that's more beneficial as well. So we talked about your emails, you do 2 a day so you 3 day promotion. You do 2-2 and then you do 3 emails, when you do you emails, do you remind your clients, your attendees that's it going to starting in an hour and then once you are live or do you just use three basic generics emails to let people know that the webinar is going to happen at a certain time.

JOSH: No, I like to hit multiply angels. So that's why I like having them build that three day window because sometimes your first angels not going to hit correctly. So you going to send one email, you see that you get about 30-40% signup right on the page, and maybe you hit a different angel, you get 50-60%. So I always like changing up those angels and trying different things and just building up the excitement for the event, and but I do usually have a base part of the email. So I only change maybe the beginning and the PS but the middle part of the email is always the medium potatoes of what's going to be covered on the webinar. So I will have three or four bullet points of what will be covered to get them excited and in the beginning of the email, is what usually what I will change up from the angel trying to get them on to the webinar.

RICH: And the subject might be.......

JOSH: Yeah and the subject plan as well, and I also leverage go to webinar for reminders emails as well. That's one thing that's very important, by default and that turned on, so you have to go and actually set them up to send 3, 6 and 24 hours in advance.

RICH: And the nice think about that is not coming out with your name. It's coming out with GoTo's name. So they don't think that you're list, don't think that you spamming them with this all kind of emails to remind them to that webinar is going to happen. I was talking with Daniel Hall and I don't know if you know this trick or not but just before the webinar starts, he usually put something in bracket, he changes the title and it will go some play starting now at then he will click on notify all participants and once he does that it just send another email again saying, Hey! We are starting now. Have you ever used that?

JOSH: Yeah, I do that all the time. It's very effective because you get that last group of people who forget about it, boom! They get that last email and they get on.

RICH: What kind of show operates you have. Let me ask you this. You don't have to be that era but give me a generic idea on how many people on your list and how many people that you mail and what is your show operate to average webinars of yours?

JOSH: Yeah I have about 55,000 people on my list right now, typically I usually get about 300-400 people live on the webinar and of course it depends on the content that's been shared. The highest I ever gotten was about 700 people was the most I've ever got but on average about 300-400 and yeah this is all about being committed and staying and just continuing to just like one regular promotion that's going on. Your list knows when you're fully committed to that promotion, same thing goes when you trying to get people on webinar.

RICH: You know I totally agree with that and you know it's always building a report with your list because actually people by people and by emotions and if you build a report with a list, they're going to trust you. So if you going to recommend this particular product, they are going to go okay! Well Josh recommends it and they must be good so I'm going to buy it. Now we're going to go ahead, we're going to start a webinar and the webinar starts at let's say 8 o clock. Do you do anything to go out of your way like for example; I like to do a pre-show, I usually open it up about

15 minutes kind of chat with my list, and then my presenter will come on and do a little bit check, and we always start on time. Do you do anything similar to that?

JOSH: Yeah, I usually start just a few minutes early, welcome everyone, get an idea I like to do where is everybody from, get an idea, all of that, maybe talk about anything happening; sports that may have happened just for a few minutes. I don't like to do too much of long kind of back-and-forth chat because then if you start recording then that's you can of act like you cut that out and do all that stuff so I usually do about 3-4 minutes of that, and then I jump right into introducing the hopes. Then I spend more time doing that and building them up, as the expert for the night so that I can pass off the authority that my list has with me over to the person that is presenting.

RICH: Now do you..... Once you start the webinar, assume that you used to, do you ever not start on time to wait for more people to come in, let's say it supposed to start at 8 o clock, the other started at 5 or 10 minutes after?

JOSH: Always, Always and that's the reason why I like to do those 2-4 minutes of that back and front to give those people, those people so ..... Last emails I starting now email, I don't give those people a chance to get on so yeah! I always make sure that I at least do usually 5-7 minutes. I like doing it in 10 minutes; you can like people that were on their early start. Hey! Why you taking so long to start?

RICH: But you did started right on time now since it supposed to be at 8 o'clock, you do 5-6 minutes prior to that and then 8 o'clock, you go ahead and start recording?

JOSH: Yeah! So I started right at 8 o'clock, I started maybe 7:57, I'll do some small talk to about 8, and then present a buildup presenter for another 3-4 minutes and then boom. I like about 8:05- 8:07, get it started officially.

RICH: Now, you go ahead and you host a webinar do you interact with the presenter or do you just say okay! Hey Josh here and here's my guest for the night Rich he's got great program. Okay Rich go! Do you do that?

JOSH: Yeah, it depends. I like to hash that before so I talk to because some people they get distracted. I mean if you jump in and then in the up they completely get off the game. So I like to find that from presenter Hey! Do you want me to interact? Do you say anything? If you do, reach out to me and be here, not just do your things so it's really going to depend on presenter. They like to interact or not because like I said, some people want to do their thing because they have everything already mapped out.

RICH: And especially if you throw them off, I get kind of torn I used to get teased a lot when I was doing webinars with JV zoo. But I would just basically basically do an intro, tell them hey, Look I am just going to be off the side and I'm going to answer the question but I'm going to mute myself, and I am going to let you go. Where's the argument I had with you Bryan, Rose, and Joel (inaudible) (20:05)? They like to get in there and jump, and that's so much interrupt but they feel like they're participating, and again the mix feeling is if you're on a flow and you know that this flow has worked, If you end up closing less people on that webinar, the first one I'm going to blame is Joel (inaudible) (20:25) and Bryan Rose for jumping in there. So you know I totally agree. So now that you've done this webinar and the webinar gets started, do you ever jump in when it's time for them... they've finished the Q&A and let me ask you this first. Do you ever work the question box? Do you help work the list or work with chat box? And try to answer questions to help the presenter?

JOSH: Always, Always! Not only if something that I can answer, I go ahead and answer right then and there. If it's something that I can't answer, its specific to whatever the presenter sharing, I will be sure to write it down and save those for the end so that we have good Q&A at the end. Because I think that's important as well to answer everyone's question. I specially pertained to whatever the offer is.

RICH: Now you mentioned you chat a little bit with the presenter prior to presenting it to your list. You actually know what your list like's and how they like it. Do you ever talk with your presenter and give them advice and how they should present their program to your list?

JOSH: I don't..... If it's something that they've ran before and they have the knowledge of a proven webinar that converts. I don't like to touch [inaudibly 21:41] this is something that you've done and you know that it works.

RICH: Right!

JOSH: Let's go ahead and run with that. If it's more of a new webinar that hasn't being proven before, I will take a look and be like, Hey! We may need to add some more proof for the beginning, some more case studies, with things like that. Just very little feedback because I don't being that person to be like "Hey we need to change your complete email webinar and this is not how you do it." So it really depends on if the webinar proven and let's roll with it.

RICH: You know I have been chatting with a lot of people doing webinar and I was just always curious, do you ever run into a guy who not only have they done the intro, but they go into their hero stories. They are going to the 'about me'. Do you ever windup having somebody who is just way too long about me, and didn't quite get into the content?

JOSH: Actually, I have never had that happen before. When I present my own webinars I like to go through as quickly as possible because people don't really care, how I feel. The people are on there, they are on there for whatever reason was e-mail to them. If they are on there because you told them they going to learn X Y Z. That's what they care about. They don't care about you know all the other stuff.

RICH: That's the other thing that I like to do. I like when somebody is going to present a webinar they have got to deliver content. Now, sometime people use this 'over deliver' concept but there is no over deliver, you either give a 100% or you don't. Do you require when somebody is going to do a webinar for you, that they deliver at least a good 45 minutes to an hour worth of the content?

JOSH: Yes, I prefer for them to deliver what they are promising to my list. So that's why I like seeing the recording before I actually decide to book the date for the webinar because I like to see what is being presented and whatever there, that's what I am going to promise my list that they are going to get. I expect for them to get that same value of whatever i saw. That's why I use that to get them on the webinar because that's telling them "Hey you are going to learn this information." That's what I expect, I expect for the promise to be delivered.

RICH: And you have to vet your webinar and I totally understand. There comes a point though when they have given all that information, and we know that most of your attendees having the attention span of 51 minutes and it's just the proven fact that after 51 minutes if you really don't get to the meet of the matter they going to go away. Now once have 51 minutes happen or let's say the people who are presenting the webinar are going too long, do you ever jump in and say "Hey what? It's time for a little bit a Q&A. Hey! I have got some questions here in the box." Do you ever participate when it comes time for Q&A and close the sale?

JOSH: I do absolutely participate because I think that's important for the person who is hosting it to come on and say "Hey this is incredible offer" and to just give that extra approval that they need to purchase that product. What I don't like doing is if someone going a little wrong, I don't like to cut in and break there flow and be like "Hey we need to stop now and go to the sale." But one thing that I do like to do is if the person is answering a lot of question and not getting back to offer. I will jump in and I will look for a question that talks about the offer, and then bring the attention back to the offer as well because sometime you can get carried away on the question and answer sections that not pertaining to the offer. So, I will like to jump in and be like "alright guys you know we only have X amount of bonuses left" are let you know this offer is only good for the next 3 days make sure you jump on it. So if there is so much unrelated Q&A going on I will bring it back, and touch the offer and stress the urgency anything like that to pick it up now.

RICH: How important is a bonus offer to you? Do you leave it up to just presenter to offer the bonus or do you jump in and give away your own bonuses as incentive for you attendees to buy now?

JOSH: Yeah 95% of the time I will go ahead and I will put ahead of my own bonus. It will be of course as relevant as possible to whatever the offer is, because I think that's important and only does this shows that I really do approval of product but it's going to help them to get better result with whatever the offer is.

RICH: And sometime people are buying bonuses they kind of forget that the product there just listen to is one that is going to solve a problem and really benefit them but it seems that's the hot button is a bonus. Now how do you handle the replays, what did you do in your replays?

JOSH: Yeah! I think that's were the most important part comes in and where truly being committed to the promotion really is important. I have had numerous times where I only make 6-7 sales live on the webinar. Most be like "Oh you know it didn't work". But if you stay committed and hit the replays you can end up making 30, 40, 50 sales in total. The majority of sales are going to come from the replays and that last 48 hours of urgency, that's where the majority of the sales come in. I hit the webinar replays as hard as I hit the buildup of the webinar. I mail two times a day and then on the closing day I mail 3 or 4 times a day.

RICH: Letting you know the webinar is up and about.

JOSH: Yeah! I think that just as important to make sure to not get too discouraged with the sales on the webinar live. Just make sure you continue the replays because that's where the majority of sales they are going to come in.

RICH: Now, have you ever run in the presenter, who is presenting your product is absolutely all wrong and you actually pulling your hair out and you want to pull the plug?

JOSH: Yeah, I had that done one time. Multiple things were happening that just made want to just pull the plug. There are always just links to eBook being put in, links to fan pages of you know telling them go to the fan page and like the page to be able to get access to free product list goes it like, and this at the end of the webinar and that few things are going on. To me at the end of the webinars should be focused on closing the sale and getting people's question answered that are on the fence about making that purchase. So anything inside of that is to me is like, what is going on, like stop talking about free stuff and get back to closing the sale.

RICH: Well, there are two folds on that, I will tell you why I'm not too crazy about that is one we hold our own GoTo because you don't really want to give up our list. Let's say for example somebody else hold their webinar and then on GoTo and you send 1500 registrants, well that 1500 people on their list, and will quite pay for that and so I disagree with them putting in on GoTo. Especially if I'm going to mail my list. The other thing is that why should these people give away the free link because even though you are entitled to my list of people that would buy the product, you are not entitled to the registrants just to build your list. So I totally disagree with somebody putting a link in PDF to get something for free. What did you think about that?

JOSH: Absolutely, I had the one bad experience like that where a guy was showing the link on the fan page, and then from the fan page there was a link. That was what was even crazier for me because the way that it happen is he was sharing the linked to his fan page and telling them to like his fan page and then scroll to the first post and the first post there was a link to the free download. So there were multiple steps in trying to get these people on to get this free thing. Then on the flip side I had another guy who wants to give away something for free and told me beforehand which was great. That was the other bad part of the other one, I didn't know that this going to happen at the end of the webinar. So the other guy did it the right way. He told me that he is going to give something for free. Which was the free PDF not only did he ask me for my affiliate link so he can embed my affiliate link in the free PDF. It also didn't require multiply steps during the webinar, during the webinar he gave away the right link to the free PDF which had my affiliate link embedded in the PDF and that's, I think if you give away anything for free, that's the right way to do it. To give away the free product, and make sure the person that's hosting your webinar has there affiliate link embedded in it. So that sales comes back to you.

RICH: Yeah, you know I agree with that because if somebody who would click on that embedded link and purchase that would be like another sale wouldn't it?

JOSH: Yeah absolutely! So not only are you giving away something for free but you are ensuring that the person hosting your webinar get credit for the new link that they clicked on in the

PDF.

RICH: So, most of the times when you host your own webinar usually the JV webinar and its usually split 50%. What is the biggest webinar that you have ever done, what the highest gross sale in the webinar that you had ever done with that?

JOSH: My highest grossing is 160,000

RICH: Wow! That tells me 80,000 for you or pretty close to that

JOSH: Yeah, Yeah!

RICH: One night?

JOSH: Yeah one night, I think I was on vacation I believe as well. So didn't do much work to it, just send up the email get people and some hit the replays.

RICH: And you what this is all from your list correct?

JOSH: Yeah, Yeah!

RICH: So you know that must be often, Awesome! You must be in demand to have people have you host their webinars. So we do the webinar so you hit it pretty hard in the beginning anywhere from twice a day to three times a day to day of webinar, and then you have 2 days' worth of the webinar replay which you hit it again twice a day and sometimes three times up to that webinar. So you are basically saying that it is a 6 day promotion?

JOSH: Yeah, Yeah! Usually the way that I do it most of time is live webinar either on the Tuesday, Wednesday or Thursday anyone of those three days actually have the live webinar and run the promotion all the way until Sunday.

RICH: Now what about follow up, let's say the people that don't buy. Do you ever get on them, and just follow up on it to see if they want one more opportunity to purchase.

JOSH: Actually no! I never done much of that usually I hit the promotion all the way until the end, and if people do email my support desk after the offer close and they still want to buy I will try in you know see if the owner or product vendor still willing to do that but that's pretty much it. I don't do much after, after the offer close to me the offer close, I mean I don't want to step on anyone's toes, I don't want to over step a boundary.

RICH: With your highest grossing webinar, what would be an average sale on my list? Let's say for example you put a 100 or a 200 people on a webinar. What is an average closing ratio now i know it sometimes depends on the presenter but let's say you have a mediocre presenter out of 100 people how many they usually sale?

JOSH: If I have a 100 people on live. I would like to have between 6-10 sales. So it's between 6-10% closing ratio, and of course it depends on the price of the offer. If it's the higher price offers then I will expect more towards the lower number 6-7 sales. If it's 297 or 497 I will expect you know 10-12 sales live on the webinar and then from there from the replays.

RICH: And what is the highest webinar that your list will hold where they have a potential of purchasing?

JOSH: I have never done more, I think the highest price point I went was $1497 that was the highest prize point that I went, and I actually there was $1497 with the split pay option as well.

RICH: 2-3 payments?

JOSH: Yeah!

RICH: Yeah, that's the way to go you don't necessary want to give your attendees, give them a chance to an absolute No! What I believe that you should give him an alternative of choice, it's going to be a thousand dollar product, 3 payments of 330 or two payments of 525 or one payment of 997. So I know I totally agree with that. So you have an average of 6-7% how often do you do these webinars. Do you do them every week? Do you do them on a certain day, and what is the good time that you think that you start a webinar or host the webinar?

JOSH: Yeah, I actually don't do many webinar. I probably do maybe one a month. Just because I really do it I believe promote it really, really hard. I will do once a week it will just, it will take a lot of out of myself and a lot of my list what is promote back hard every time for a webinar. So I like to do one a month, and my ideal time is usually about 3-4 pm. That's usually the time I like to have my webinar. I just find it to be a good time, usually sometime when they get too later in the day people that is in another country somewhere in Europe its get a little late in the day for them, and people here in the US usually about 3-4 pm its good time I feel that people in US can still get on regardless of where they are.

RICH: Have you split tested that? Because I know I like to do my webinar at 7-8 o'clock at night eastern standard time?

JOSH: No, I have never split tested it much at all. I guess it's just a time that I have been in a custom to doing.

RICH: Now, did you ever have somebody repeat a webinar? Do you do encore performance that's live or do you just go right to the reply and then promoted it such?

JOSH: I've had people ask me to doing encore but if the sales are rolling with the webinar replays and It's working the webinar replays working lets I am just going to closer hard on the last day with the urgency scared from all my side. So I have been asked to do encore. I have never actually done one. So I mean I am open to it but if to me personally if the webinar replay selling me well. I know that last day we can do well regardless because I have the urgency at the scarcity on my side.

RICH: Right, That's awesome! When you go out and you solicit other people for your other webinars, do you have a big list of JV's that do webinar that will fit your list, and how do you approach them?

JOSH: Yeah, One of the reason why I haven't being doing many of my webinars on my own is because I have approached some people that I felt would do well with my webinar and then for some reason they don't fully commit to the promotion. So although they promote and get the people on live, only do about 5-6 sales and then think 'oh, this is not going to be a good webinar', and they drop the promotion instead of continuing it continuing up to closing because I tell them look "this is normal just continues pushing them and ends up 30-40 sales and this is the way it works."

RICH: Well 30-40 sales, what price point do you usually....

JOSH: Usually about between, I usually offer 497 to 997 so yeah, that's what I tell them to stick with it and I am good on sales but some people just like moving on.

RICH: I don't understand that because that tells me its $250 - $500 a wax. When I go ahead and push it get one more sales, that's a one more sale, its 500 bucks.

JOSH: Yeah, Yeah that's literally. So have about 3-4 those back to back in a row. It took a lot of energy out of me because especially doing live webinars for me it's really exhausting like. I'm on there for an hour and half or 2 hours by the time end of it, I am just exhausted and I don't want to do anything else. I am going to be doing more actively, going out there and pursuing more JV's but I always just time period for my 3-4 people and where that happen that situation happen and always drain time draining and empty drain.

RICH: Alright! Do you ever... Do you ever when you going out and promoting your own webinar I mean you in SEO guy you are a video guy, do you ever use a video or SEO or do you buy Facebook ads in other to put people into the seats on your own webinars.

JOSH: Yeah! Since a webinar is usually short time period, so 3 or 4 days kind of build up to the live webinar I prefer just going on and buying the traffic that is a lot quicker, sometime the SEO can take specially ranking the video can take you know week to week and half to get that video ranked. So I want to get traffic by the way, Boom! I usually just pay for it and run video ads or run you know regular image ads on Facebook, and also run some re-targeting running ads. That's usually my goal too when I really want to get people on the webinar.

I just go on and pay for it.

RICH: How much do you usually spend when you do Facebook ads or targeting ads?

JOSH: I usually buy about 20 buck a day's up until we go live.

RICH: Have you ever thought of scaling it up and maybe experimenting maybe spending $100 or $200 you got a price point for $497 and $997 why wouldn't you spend a $1000 to try to put a thousand people in their seats?

JOSH: Yeah! Good point, never done more than $20 bucks a day. But absolutely that's a good point.

RICH: So when you are doing $20 bucks a day and doing the re-targeting I'm imaging that you specifically go after an audience. What $20 bucks a day bring you, if you do three day's at $20 bucks that's $60 bucks instead of a 100. How many people there is put in the seats?

JOSH: With retargeting that traffic is usually a lot cheaper it can get me about 1000-2000 clicks to the registration page. So assuming the registration page converts the same 30% that's anywhere between 300-600 people this to the registration to the webinar.

RICH: Exactly, Exactly! Here's is another thing to even through you are getting you paying for these clicks, and you are spending really a very little amount of money that's also going to build your list as well and you said you have like 55,000 people on your list. How effective when it comes to constantly showing up for your webinars?

JOSH: Yeah, I mean I usually always on average I get about 300-

400 per webinar. So since I only do one a month. Usually that number pretty consistent and like if it does the duller or lower I go ahead and promote harder. I think that one of the reason why for me it's pretty consistent to get 300-400 people on because I don't do that many, and its surprisingly it's tough to find may people that can get over 100 people live on a webinar just because I mean you know one thing for one reason or another it's not that popping it for people to be able to get it on a live webinar.

RICH: And it takes a bloomy, it takes a lot for mail to JV zoo, we male are entire list which is about 200,000 people. So we can get 700-800 people on a webinar but still we are burring our own list because the JV zoo we want to have out list that buy our product of the day. Because you know when it comes down too it weren't affiliate as well. But one we take the time to mail out for a webinar it just for some reason it start to burn the list, and it's never as effective on the other hand, we are printing 700 people in the seats. That's usually the grantees anywhere between $50-75 or $100 products. Now I seeds start about $497. I know you mentioned 497 and 997 do you find that you convert more and 497 rather than 997.

JOSH: Yes, I have personally like that $497 sweet spot just because many time people with that $497 sweet you get away without having an offer a split payment option just because people find it a lot more affordable with the $997 you going to get a lot more people requesting a split payment option. If you are not offering yet, so I prefer that $497

RICH: What kinds of tips or tricks or hack do you have that not only helps to increase the attendance of your webinar but perhaps your closing ratio as well, anything?

JOSH: Yeah, absolutely one of the greatest things again is been 100% committed to the promotion. Do this from the very beginning; make sure you email multiply times a day and find different angels to get people to come to the webinar, make sure that you know what's going to be, make sure you are knowledgeable on what the webinar going to be covering also you can build it up to get people on the webinar, and also make sure you always set those 'go to' host webinar reminders so that they automatically getting reminded because I thought that they were turned on automatically

RICH: Like what they aren't!

JOSH: Yeah, you have to actually go in there and turn them on. Like you said make sure that you can run the 'go to' webinar promotion on your account, so that you are in full control, your email list still in your full control or they are people that pretty much unlike either rent there go to webinar account. I know Demin roofice, I sure you know Demin Roofice yeah, he runs a service and I thinks its 97 or 127 and let you host your webinar through his account for you that way your leads are not compromised.

RICH: Well, you are exactly. I spend $87 a month. I loved to rent to go webinar.

JOSH: Yeah, Yeah! Absolutely!

RICH: Do you write your copy? Are you a copy writer?

JOSH: Yeah, I like write my own stuff. I like to write my own emails just because I feel more comfortable, I tried outsourcing my email copying before it does feel the same. It feels like my voice, so I've read tons of copy writing books continue goggling myself. So I don't offer copywriter service, Copy writing as a service but I love doing that for myself. It's just something I just like riding of stuff that sells.

RICH: Do you use auto responder? Do you use a Webber?

JOSH: Yeah, I actually use A. Webber, I use mail jet and I have a get responsive account as well.

RICH: Got you! Well, we offer to get responsive account on JV zoo but you know I have mixed feeling about that the open rates and the way even a Webber get response. It's seems to me that they might be going into the spam a little more than often. Marine and I talking about (Inaudible) (45:10) Entrisick Tronic, are you familiar with Entrisick Tronic?

JOSH: I've seen it, I've seen people using it but I have never done Entrisick Tronic.

RICH: What about confusion software, they thought about using?

JOSH: I've did have an account with them because they Demin Roofice he is a big support of confusion software but I got in there, not pretty confusing for me.

RICH: I think that's why they called confusion software and so I like to keep it simple, there is at all thing, keep it simple same, and the simpler you can keep it the more money you are going to make and less issue that you going to have. Josh thanks so very much for coming on to this program. You know it's very appreciated we known each other a long time, and I am glad that we had this time to chat. I'm very amazed that you know you did $160,000 on a webinar which goes to show that if you get the right webinar and if you build it right you get the people on the seats and proper closing techniques are used. You can make that $80,000 a night for a pay cheque and that's pretty awesome.

JOSH: One last thing that I want to share about that webinar. One thing that really I think will help close a lot of sales that night was the presenter, he did something very genius that can be very helpful at the end when we are doing Q&A. He's not only answering the question that the normal question that's coming in, but he did something very unique at the end. He said ''if you are on the fence about purchasing this offer in the chat box, I want you to write 'on the fence' and then put your question next to it.'' So that was genius to me. He was getting everyone that was thinking about purchasing the offer to write a question why they are not buying yet? And then he would answer just those questions, and that was genius.

RICH: And that's basically what sale is all about. You have to overcome all the objection and once you overcome all the objections there should be no reason why they cannot purchase. My two favorite words when I am delivering a webinar and okay So we answered this question, we have answered that question are there any more question, and then I usually say other than that is there any reason stopping you for purchasing this now? Go ahead and write it in question box or write in the chat box and once you do that and you address people by name and they go you know what 'Josh I understand how it feel, and most people felt that way until they use that product and it solved the problem and once all problem got solved they justifies the cost is that what you are looking for josh? It is well awesome! Go ahead and click on the buy link and welcome to the family.'

JOSH: I loved that, loved that.

RICH: And then you got another sale hopefully!

JOSH: Yeah, absolutely he kept doing that because every time we did that more sales started coming in, more sales start coming in. He didn't stop until finally sales stop coming in then it was genius. Another thing that he did that always amazing as well was at the very start of the webinar he started with just go to webinar and a lot of just share your camera. Yeah, your webcam Boom! He starts very personal. Hey guys, this is me Boom! We both started with sharing our face gave people that personal touch or it can actually see.

RICH: Yeah! The only bad thing about that is it isn't recorded. At recording you not going to get that face, so going to have that personality Ricky Catcher is that who you talking about?

JOSH: No! No! It was Chris Recerd.

RICH: Oh yeah! Chris Recerd is pretty awesome! Oh yeah, he is somebody that I going to be interviewing as well for who you know for 50k

JOSH: He gets some tips.

RICH: Yeah, that's awesome. Josh! Thank you so very much to taking your time today. I know you're a very busy guy and I do appreciate. It's all going to be part of my *50k webinar blueprint*, and it's an honor and a privilege to have you on, and thank you so very much.

JOSH: Thank you Rick!

RICH: Oh! you very welcome, and for of you who still with us thank you so very much for taking part in this program please watch for the book and don't forget to take care of you when it comes to doing webinar's take these tips and tray and use them and make yourself a great webinar. So on behalf of everybody here a 50k webinar a blueprint. I want to thank you very much to come and bye and we will see you later.

Karl Schuckert

Rich: Hello everybody and welcome to the 50k webinar blueprint. My name is Rich Wilens, thank you very much for taking your time out of your very special time today for me and for you and for our guest today. This is the 50k webinar blueprint, everybody who we have on our program basically make $50,000 plus on one webinar, that's right, and today we're going to be talking with my friend and somebody who I also just did a webinar with, we did over 50,000. Please welcome to the program Karl Schuckart. Karl, welcome to the program.

Karl: Thank you, I'm excited to be here.

Rich: I'm glad to you here too. This is going to be a great opportunity for everybody who's not only reading this book but who's also interested in webinars and how lucrative it is for you to do a webinar and I know the webinar we just did recently was very lucrative, in fact today thank you very much because I received another little bonus check in the mail for about... well I can't really say what it is but it was a bonus, it was very good so I want to thank you very much for that.

So tell me about it Karl, how did you get involved in webinars and what do you do in your webinar that makes you so successful.

Karl: It really came down to training and being fully immersed and focused to be sort of like an actor in a sense, and I learned at a kind of a young age, I've been a sales trainer for a long time, I actually was in the insurance industry, before that I was a door knocker knocking on doors selling security systems and at a young age I knew that I wanted to be in sales and I was good at sales as a kid selling candy bars at school, I actually had arcade games, I had my own arcade business when I was 14 years old, me and my grandma were partners. She was like one of the best sales people I've ever met and my grandpa was one of the most wealthiest guys in Texas at one point in his life, and between the both of them they had a lot of influence for me as a kid, and I literally had seen my grandpa go from dead broke to multimillionaire to dead broke again to multimillionaire, so I've seen that that can also be a vicious cycle, and so I've learned by other people's experiences at a young age.

Fast-forward a little bit, once I got into the insurance industry I really started to focus on like who are the people, who are the leaders that are teaching people how to sell, people like Tom Hopkins, ZigZiglar, The Great's Arthur, Sandler, and I just started reading their books.

I'm big at reading books and I know Rich you just wrote a book that I phenomenal, that's going to help people with doing webinars, and I also know a little about your background being into sales and being a sales trainer as well, so I know you could cope with that, but it really just comes down to training and being prepared and what really actually helped me fast-forward even further is I became a regional director for a very large insurance company and was a sales trainer on a national basis, and it all became because of processes, it became not just from books that I read but also from mentorship that I got and also some training that I got that helped me overcome the fears of public speaking.

I already understood the sales process and then I had to understand that look selling to masses is a different ballgame, selling to a group of people is a different ballgame than selling to an individual person but the same concepts, the same principles worked.

So like using tie down questions like "does that make sense, is that fair, pretty neat, huh?" like having tie down and loaded questions that get people to say yes, that's kind of where that came from and then also just following people that were really good at presentations, I literally would just go and listen to presentations not even to buy anything, I would just go there to take my notepad and listen to like how are they doing sales, how are they getting the crowd involved and then also how involved does the crowd seem to be?

So I would really pay attention to the actual psychology of sales and what's actually going on through the process and then I would also pay attention to myself like do I feel giddy, do I feel excited, am I ready to buy?

And so I would just pay attention to a lot of that stuff. So it came back, going back to the question, so it really came back as a kid, kind of getting myself ready knowing that I wanted to be in sales and then having good mentors, reading good books, there's a book out there called "Question Based Sales", I don't have the author's name. I was actually looking for it but that's a highly recommended book because it actually teaches you how to find the question that your audience is looking for to buy that product, what's the biggest that they have and then how do you formulate that into a presentation, and so that's part of it.

Rich: You know, it's funny that you mentioned that because you mentioned The Great's, I started working with Tom Hopkins back in 1976 Scottsdale Arizona where I actually became the sales closer that I am today, and you talk about books, the one that I happen to have right here you see this guy right here, Grant Cardone.

A little story about Grant Cardone, when I was doing sales training for the automobile field back in the 80's, Grant actually attended one of my workshops, he attended twice one of my workshops and one time I even gave him a ride to the airport, and you know, he said he's going to be this big sales trainer and he appreciated me, appreciated, Jack B. Cooper and he appreciated the Great's that you were talking about, Tom Hopkins, ZigZiglar, Joe Girard for the automobile business, all of these people were closers and you know even though this book is the closer's guide it's very important for you not only to learn those tie down questions but to ask the questions, and what it really comes down to is eliminating all the objections and one you eliminate all the objections you have to ask for the sales.

I understand exactly where you're coming from and it's funny that you mentioned the arcade game, you must have liked counting a lot of quarters because I remember playing pong for hours and I remember taking these quarters and putting them into the machine in my favorite... I can't even remember what my favorite was but it wasn't Mario brothers but it was back in the day.

Karl: Asteroids?

Rich: It was asteroids, you're absolutely correct, so asteroids was one of my favorites so that as pretty awesome.

So you worked from the insurance business all the way to the internet marketing business, tell me Karl, how did you get started in the internet marketing?

Karl: So being in the insurance industry there was some ups and downs, like I said I was a regional director for a large insurance company and I was happy there that I was working like 80-100 hours a week, my day started at 6am and didn't end till like 1pm at night, every single day and even weekends I was with the people I was mentoring to become great at sales constantly, and so it was great, don't get me wrong, the experiences were great, the leadership was amazing with the company I was with.

So I had something really great that I was with but something happened in the corporate structure that I didn't really agree with and so I had to make a change and so I actually left the company; me and my now wife, we moved down to San Diego, we didn't know what we were doing but we just wanted to move to San Diego, we wanted to get out of Vegas which is where we were running our company, an so we went down there and we like literally crashed, like the stock market crashed, black Monday and all that stuff, that's what it felt like to me in my life at that point and it was actually late 2007, 2008 was the year everything crashed anyways, so I was definitely affected by that and I was just kind of like burned out on insurance, kind of sick of talking about death all the time because of selling life insurance and you can only talk about that so much and help people if it's a very emotional thing but it's a very intangible thing too, so you have to be good at selling something that's intangible.

But basically fell on my face, we were living in like 800sq ft. apartment, we were basically going to like a food bank and were basically begging, I was calling my grandpa for money and borrowing money from him all the time.

It was a really bad place in my life, but what happened from it was, because of the skills that I had from the insurance company, I said you know what?

I'm just going to start my own insurance brokerage, and I was listening to a lot of the online guys like Mike Filsaime, Russell

Brunson and a few others like Mike Koenigs and stuffs like that.

I was really listening to them and I was trying to be a part of them, there was another guy, I've forgotten his name but basically following these guys for all my life, figuring out how they're doing it, listening to the guys that are doing marketing not just doing sales and basically just reformulated their presentation, went online, was one of the first brokers online to sell contracts to independent agents, and because of that Google actually gave our company a very high remark so we had no problem with recruiting people.

I still own the company, I still actually own an insurance brokerage company that does 7 figures a year. I actually built a company that was able to afford me to look for something else because I was completely bored with that industry,

I must say I was very bored with the insurance industry, it's a boring topic, it really is, but lucrative. I still have it but what I did is I automated everything I possibly could because of the stuff I learned from internet marketing and about 4 and half years ago almost 5 years ago now I went to an even that Russell Brunson was having and I had one meeting with him and that meeting changed the course of my life at that point, because I knew that I wanted to jump into something else, I knew that I wanted to jump into the internet marketing world, and I asked him one question, I said, "Hey, how do I get into this industry, this is my background, it's offline, my background is completely offline, I've taken it and I've automated it somewhat online and the rest of it is offline; offline selling,"

Russell goes, "Well, that's what you're good at, right?" and I was like yes, that's what I'm good at, and he goes, "well why don't you just do something about that, like teach people how to sell insurance on a bigger level" and then the light bulb hit. So right at that point I jammed home, I'm like I'm bored, I hate this stuff, I hate to say that but I really was just bored with the industry, but i had so much knowledge, I had so much I could give to people that are new in that industry and trying to get into it and so what I did is I created a site called finalexpenseprogram.com and it's a full training site that teaches people.

I took my presentation, I've got tons of video training on there and I did everything completely white hat, built a podcast, built a YouTube channel, did a Udmamy course, like a free course, did a whole free thing, took the whole photo ideas and created a funnel, didn't spend a dime on advertising, it was all white hat.

Basically, that was my exit, so 4 and half years ago that was my exit, that was when I had my light bulb, that when I decided that the internet marketing industry is where I belonged and then I went to a JVZoo event shortly after that and so the game was over once I went to a JVZoo event, I met everybody, met you there Rich. You were one of the first people I met actually.

Rich: I think I was at the registration table when you walked up and I said how do you spell your name?

Karl: Yeah, you were.

Rich: And which one was that, was that when we had Orlando there?

Karl: No, San Diego.

Rich: I'm glad you showed up, in fact I think I remembered you showed up as part of Chris Record's posse. Is that correct?

Karl: No, there's a a backstory on that, that's my mentor. So I've had millionaire mentors and Chris Record is the latest millionaire mentor that I've had. Chris showed up with his posse, he was like untouchable, like when I went there I didn't know anybody, I knew a few people, I met like Jay Cruise, him and I are really good friends and I hung out with everybody, I hung out with Mike Filsaime when I was there, I hung out with the people I was looking up to like Ben Adkins and stuff like that.

Really looked up to these guys, watching them, I'm not a start struck type of person but I was great for me to finally say like you're human and I'm human, we're real people and it was a very pivotal time for me and I did everything I could to possibly network with these people and keep I touch with them, so I did not meet Chris there.

I did see Chris there, I did introduce myself to him but he was flying through everywhere he went, like he was kind of hard to go and talk to. What happened with Chris was, and this like my way of hacking mentorship from people that you look up to is make a list of all the people you look up to and then geographically look at where have they lived and how close are they in proximity from where you live and then do multiple ways to get in touch with them.

So with Chris I actually contacted him on Facebook because he's a Facebook guy so that wasn't hard. He actually responded from Facebook and said hey, what's up and I said, "Hey Chris, I noticed you live close to me, you're within an hour or two away from where I live, I've seen that you are close by, I really look up to you, I really respect you and I just want to give you a shout out" and he was like oh man, thanks, that's really cool....

So I said you know what, I've got these skills, I've spent the last 3 and a half years at that point learning SEO, learning Facebook traffic, learning how to build websites, how to build funnels.

I was learning all those skills, I knew that I needed to have those skills in order for me to get into this industry and so I came in with skills, so I would say you have to have skills before you do this. But I told him that hey I would love to work with you, if there is anything I can do, I would love to just come in and be a fly on the wall or learn from you and be friendlier and Chris goes, "huh, interesting".

So then he started qualifying me, he said what do you have, what are your skills, what can you do, what can you bring to the table, and I threw up on the table everything that I could do, and then he said you know what?

Come into the office tomorrow or the next day, it was quick, things happened quickly. So come in the next day and let's just see what happens, I can guarantee you anything but let's just see what happens, I was like ok, cool. I went there and we became great friends.

Rich: He's a great guy, you know

Karl: Yeah, he is, he's a very open person, it's sometimes hard to get a hold of him for people because he literally has, I've seen it, he has hundreds and hundreds people pounding his door, I'm just one that happened to get through and then once I got through our friendship kind of grew from there, and so I had skills, it's what I said you have to have some skill set, you can't be a complete newbie and knock on an internet marketer's door and say I'm willing to do anything to work for you to get those opportunities, and literally for a year I worked pretty hard for Chris being unknown, nobody knew who as but I worked my ass off to help him grow his business and definitely feel like I was a part of it, so it's a cool thing, it's a cool feeling to know

Rich: And you know, I remember when LA or Vegas.

Karl: It was in Vegas.

Rich: Oh yeah, that's right [16:22] I knew right then that you were a guy that really had his act together. So tell me, [16:31], what made you decide to do webinars? Because you and I did a very successful webinar just a few weeks ago, did it just come to you in a light bulb or say webinars, that's the thing?

Karl: Well I'm really big on preplanning stuff and actually going to a white board, writing out, when we did our webinar had just gotten done doing Chase Bowers product which was the shopified app, and Chase built an app, he was actually Interest record's 7 figure traffic academy mastermind and he started polling people in the room about a product and he actually built a product based off of everybody's needs that were in drop shipping that were using shopify, and he was using it, my wife was dabbling in it and so I've seen the product.

He built a beta version and he invited everybody to use it, so I saw the product and I was like this is a product that I've got to get behind, I was already helping Chris Records do launches as a JV broker, I helped him with the smart member 1.0 and 2.0, I helped with the speed blogging extension that he did.

So I was already helping him, I was already getting kind of to know the industry; I was cutting my teeth, right? So basically at that point I saw Chase's product, I knew that I wanted to get onboard and so I contacted Chase and I said Chase, loved the product, want some help launching it? And I think I can do a good job for you.

So basically I knew that I had to believe in the product before I'm going to be like a JV broker, and so Chase was like sure, come onboard let's see what you can do. So with Chase what I was able to do because of my background was help him build a phenomenal funnel, in fact I remember you contacting me going, what the heck are you selling, the funnel is closing like 60% and it even got higher than that because of the way we designed it, it's actually really cool the way we designed it, we have a whole case study that we put together, haven't really released it yet but real soon, and so basically it's based off for me how well a product performs.

So if the launch is like a really good deal for people to get in, that's why I love JVZoo by the way because it gives small businesses the opportunity to buy products before they actually go mainstream because there's a lot of products that actually go and have the potential to go mainstream, so that product was a product to me that I felt like could actually go mainstream.

So basically took that product and basically leveraged it, and when I saw the conversions were so good I was like this would be a perfect webinar product, I knew right away that we could actually sell this on webinar. I already was helping Chris with some webinars like him and Andrew Graham would set a lot of webinars, I would go on and see how they would sell their products and it would sell.

I think they had a webinar that like $350,000, so they had some of the highest converting products or highest converting webinars that I have seen and because of some of that mentorship that I got from Chris I was ready, I mean I was pretty much as ready to do a webinar, and so when we talked I was like hey we have a webinar if you want to do it and you were like yeah let's do it but you better perform, and I was like yeah I know, I would.

Rich: I remember telling you that because my butt was on the line too, I was recommending you. Well let's jump right into this, ok?

When you are preparing for a webinar, what is the first thing that you do, and let's go through it step by step because this is very important, even before the emails, the preparation, what is it that you do to prepare and prepare to have a very successful webinar, we're talking a 50k+ webinar?

Karl: So knowing your butt, my butt is on the line I had to perform. Not only that, but anything like when I was in the insurance industry I was used to speaking in crowds, I actually had to speak to people every single day, so my fear of speaking in a group setting is not that much, I mean we all do get butterflies no matter what but like they say in show business the show must go on, right?

So you have to be ready, you have to be ready like ready, camera, action, lights, go, you have to be ready, you have to prepare yourself. If you're not prepared you're going to be just a babbling banshee that doesn't know what the heck they're talking about. So what I do is, I actually have a little way or formula that I've come together because this is something I've written my presentations and scripts with on the insurance industry.

The webinars are a little bit different like I said, it's kind of like a comedian going to a live audience, they have to read the audience, they have to kind of know what the audience is doing. So the first thing I do and this is like NLP training is I try to pre-frame, I want to pre-frame the best as I can the people that are on the call, like I know Rich you did a little bit of that for us when you were live on the call, but other webinars that I've done I'm usually the guy that opens up the call and the excited guy, I'm the more hippie kind of person, I'm getting people aroused, my goal is to know the audience, so like when we did JVZoo, I knew that going into it that most of the people weren't going to be econ people, I realized that most of the people are going to be digital marketers or people that are following or doing digital marketing or are going to be complete newbies that are just trying to figure out their way.

So I knew that going in, so knowing that going in kind of helps you with your audience, so once I knew that then I could put a presentation out, then I could actually put a presentation together that would actually help sell people, help educate people make to a buying decision because that's really my way, it's educating, giving people the right information they need to make an educated decision and then get those questions.

So I would start the presentation out like, "hey guys, this is Karl Schuckart", very excited, right? So I'm very excited, "This is Karl Schuckart and I'm here with my guest or I'm here with my partner so and so and we've got something big for you guys, we've got something exciting for you, we've got something that you're going to absolutely love, in fact the last people that we talked to…" I was pre-framing, then I would start saying ok guys one thing that I- before that I would do something were, let's do some house cleaning, let's get people in the right state of mind to listen because I want them to open up their minds.

I want them open up their ears and I want them to open up what they're thinking about in other for them to listen and digest what we have to say, and something that l learned from Chris was serve first sell second, so always serve value first before you sell somebody something, and also from Mike Filsaime and Andy Jenkins they had a thing that they said, the 3 T's; teach, transcend transact. So you teach them first, you transcend them and then you transact. So everything that I do is based off of that along with tie down questions, along with participations, "so hey guys give me a one, give me a yes, guys are you excited learn what this is about, are you getting that, isn't that pretty cool, isn't that neat?" then I start using words like can you imagine what it would be like when you start your store, can you imagine what's going to be like after you get this information and you start applying it, and these principles that have been proven for years and they start coming back to you, stuff like that.

So I do that upfront, I do a lot of pitching and getting everybody excited about it, and then I do some things like hey guys, if you stay till the end we've got a gift for you, it's a $100 value, in fact let me just give you a peek of it, sometimes I'll pick their interest about it because I want to have them stay throughout the whole presentation, and then I tell them hey guys, look. I do these things where, I think Sandler teaches this and it's where I ask for permission to sell them something.

That is huge, whoever that's watching this, this is big, this is where my webinar convert at a max value because once you've gotten permission from people then their guards have dropped down. So I tell them upfront guys I'm not here to get you something that you don't need or want or anything like that, so I drop those guards down and then I get permission like hey, after we give you this information, after we teach and we give you some information and you're educated about this industry, is it fair that I actually have an offer for you at the end and as long it's a high value, low cost, low interest point, low barrier point for you to get into and jump into with no risk, is that fair that I actually do that for you? I've never gotten a no from that, I haven't done a lot of webinars either but I've never gotten a no. I'm even surprised every time I do because I'm like yes yes yes yes and I like getting people into the yes mode.

Rich: Exactly. Let's do a little bit of a recap of what you just talked about. You talk about not only entertaining the clients or the attendees who have shown up but you're getting them ready, you're getting them excited because nothing creates more of a sales or buying atmosphere than getting people excited about what it is that you're going to do.

Also, because I know this from hosting a lot of webinars it's like the front guy before Johnny Carson came out, oh my God, did I just say Johnny Carson, before any of those guys come out, you know you always have the warm up guys, so exactly what you were talking about. If you're going to host a webinar you've got to make sure that the excitement is there, that you're creating the excitement, that you're getting the people ready to know that not only, what you talked about what Andy Jenkins and Mike Filsaime said and what Chris preaches is that you're getting ready to deliver a value. See, some webinars that I've been on they don't deliver a value, they don't anything but 33 minutes worth of about me, 10 minutes worth of content and you want to buy this now.

What you said is very important and that's why I wanted to recap it, that you've got people excited, most importantly you got people to participate by hitting one or hitting yes. It's very important to get their participation early because once they start participating they start doing the things that you tell them to do and then to recap again, Karl you ask them for permission, you know at the end of this we have a sponsor, there's going to be an offer and if you really think that we've delivered on our promise, that we over delivered on value that you're going to have an opportunity to get those wonderful product.

Do you all agree in giving the permission for to go ahead, will you stick around till the end? And then to recap again you said I'm going to give them a little bit of something. So you entice them in order to stick around to the end of the webinar.

Did I do a fair job in recapping what it is you do?

Karl: Yes absolutely. My goal regardless if they buy or not is to provide them a ton of value that they get something out of the call and so that way they want to stick through it, they want to stick on the call and usually the free gift is usually a cool thing for people to have, like for the shopified app we gave a chrome extension and people loved it.

Rich: It's funny you mentioned that. I'm going to Chris Record's program right now; I'm a big fan of Chris. He was talking about a chrome extension today and my girlfriend Marie says, "What is a chrome extension" and I felt I should know that and I didn't. So she Goggled it and then the next thing you know it's an extension that does some cool things. So it's very important that you give away that cool thing, I know somebody who gave away one of those mini boom boxes, so I mean you're absolutely right. So we've just gone ahead and we've got things prepared. Karl how did you know that this was going to be a 50k webinar?

Karl: Actually going into it I didn't know, I wasn't sure how big we were going to do it. I knew that there were going to be a good amount of people that would join the audience especially with JVZoo, you know, I would imagine they have a pretty good list, so we what? Like 460 people I think on the call live. That's kind of an indication, I know there's a standard wording verbiage they use in the industry like how many dollars per head do you average?

And if you can average anything over 50 I think you're doing good. I was excited, when we did this I knew that the offer was going to convert no matter what, the product sells itself, of course having a guy like me that can pitch is helpful and it's going to do a good job but even if you had a boring guy show the product it probably still would have converted, it definitely wouldn't have converted a 50,000, it probably would have been like 25,000.

So you have to have a god product, you have to have a sellable product and after the success of the launch, the actual closing percentages, I didn't look at necessarily all the volume of traffic that came in, I looked at what were the closing percentages of the product.

I mean we had just a fantastic plan, the plan of how we launched it worked out so well, it brought people back into the funnel constantly the way we did it, and so knowing that we had such high conversion rate I knew that we had a great product to do webinars with, in fact we still do it.

Rich: Let's talk about a percentage. What is the percentage? Back in the old days, this is actually current now, if you're a baseball player and you're hitting 300 you're considered a superstar, so that tells me if you break it down to the power of 10 so to speak.

3 out of 10 and you're a superstar in baseball, that means if you close 3 or 30% of your attendees, so you've got a figure, if you scale it up, you have a 100 attendees you're going to close 30 people. 30 people at an average gross would be so many dollars, so analytics are very important.

But I wanted to ask you specifically about that webinar do you happen to know the total of what you made just from the live event and from the replay?

Karl: Well I know we didn't run a replay and just the live event did $58,000 in sales.

Rich: Oh yeah, you want to know why we didn't run a replay? I think it was because, it was either me, I probably should admit this but I think I didn't do the replay or something happened, there was a glitch, but with that being said, $58,000 is a lot of money. When you usually do a webinar and a replay runs, what is your typical return on the replay?

Karl: The replay is anywhere from double to triple the number that we do on the call. Today it's a little bit harder to get 100-500 people on the call live unless you have a monster list, you have a monster following, and a lot of people they just simply can't make the time you're doing a live call and typically in the game a lot of people are going to do a first webinar and like a second webinar.

The first webinar is usually a little bit soft, more educating and not necessarily pitching so much and then in the second webinar is more of a recap and then kind of closing, a little bit hard closing on the end of it because it's like the last chance to get people to get out of their sit and make a decision if they're going to buy or not. I was just saying there's a replay that's going on for the first one and there's replays that go on for the second one and usually after the second one you're going to have anywhere from double to triple the sales that you have because so many more people are going to be able to watch that replay.

Rich: Now one of the techniques that I try to teach or I want to share with people is not only do you do a live call but you can also do a live encore.

Sometimes you do it at 8 O'clock eastern standard time and then your encore is going to be at 12 noon the next day. Then from there you can do a replay, of course you mail out for the replay and then like you said you can double, triple even quadruple, so your 50,000 turns into a 150,000 or 200,000.

Let me ask your opinion, when you're doing your own mailing, when you're doing your own list, let's say I come to you with a webinar and I want you to mail your list, your customers, how many emails do you send out?

Do you have a sequence of emails or a plan that you do in order to put people on the call live?

Karl: Yes, so there are two different ways that that usually works. It depends on who the vendor is, some of the vendors don't want to send traffic to my landing page, like I might have a landing page for the webinar where we control everything, we get the leads, they go into a landing page that's proven to be high converting with jargon and stuff that's going to kind of get them ready, there's going to be a free gift, then there is a video after that, then there're about 5 emails until the day of the webinar, and then that day there's usually two or three reminding them what time it's going to be, and also too we use like sms, messenger and stuff like that too.

So it just helps with getting more people onto that live call, that's one way. The other way is just letting the vendor load up their own webinar and figuring out how they're going to get people on.

Rich: For those of you who are listening, one of the reasons why the vendors don't like to have other people hold the call or use their own platform is because it's their list and the registration usually will far more exceed the attendees. For example, with the JVZoo list and one of the reasons why we hold our own we could get anywhere between 1500 and 2200 registrations and 500 or 600 people will show up. Well if we let somebody else go ahead and do their own goto or their registration that means you're going to get 2200 people on your list and how valuable is the list?

Do you know what I mean?

Karl: Yeah. You take someone like Chris Record indoctrinated his list so well to who he is, it makes more sense too for him to actually host us on webinar versus us trying to have him send leads to our landing page and us getting a bunch of leads, obviously it's a lot of leads but there's also a point where some people like setting up backend webinars for people like in JVZoo you can have an auto register form already built into the buyers, they're automatically registered into getting on the webinar, but there's a lot of people in the launching industry that we've found that they're not good at webinars, for whatever reason it's not their thing, they don't even like to be on camera, but they're good at launching products, they're good at building software, they have guy that's usually doing the VSL (video sales letters) or they have a guy that's doing the pitching, there's a lot of guys who do that and then they're just not good on webinars.

So they host a webinar, at the end they're like so and so and I've got so and so and then it's up to us to like bring it in, bring in the game, so it's interesting.

So that's why sometimes it's good for us to have something on our end that's allowing us to go hey look, I know obviously you're going to give us some of your leads by doing this but we're doing a better job than you probably could, so we're going to have prior attendee rates, we're going to have prior opt-in rates than you're going to get and then we're going to get higher sales which is ultimately going to make you more money.

So it definitely depends, it depends, like JVZoo obviously it makes sense to them to host it on webinars, when you're Chris Record it makes more sense for you to host your own webinars.

Rich: Exactly. Now, we were talking about hosting a webinar, you mentioned earlier that you're a JV broker and you mentioned Chase Bowers, so do you also host other people's webinars and when you do host other people's webinars do you structure it for them and tell them or show them what it is that you want that knows what's going to convert and do they actually listen to you and do they do it?

Karl: Yeah, I'm still pretty new but for Chase I pretty much put the presentation together, he cleaned it up a little bit but basically I'm a man of many talents, so I can build sales letters, I can build presentations, I can build funnels for launches, I can look at a product and break the product down say this needs to be in the frontend, this is how this needs to be built it needs to look like, these are what the down sales are going to look like, here is what our backend needs to look like and so as a JV broker I have those talents, I have those skills, and so basically because of that I can help but it just depends, again I'm still pretty new in this world, I'm just forging my way in but I'm coming in with skills.

Rich: Well I have an webinar program if you need a little bit help with those skills maybe we could work something out.

Karl: Sure.

Rich: You know, I'm really excited to have you on here because you're a little bit different, you're new to this. When you do your own webinars do you spend any money, do you do any Facebook ads or any SEO or do you run Google ads? What do you do other than rely on somebody's mailing list in order to build the attendance on your webinar?

Karl: If I am doing someone else's webinar without my list or anything like that we'll do a retargeting campaign. We're running the webinar, we're running the landing page and everything, we'll actually do a retargeting campaign with our free product like hey join the webinar you'll get a free product. We have a video that we've already made; we've got carousel ads that we've already made and stuff like that.

So it will actually drive people back into- if they haven't. We put a conversion pixel on the thank you page and then we have a pixel on the first page that's retargeting them on Facebook, so we're following them around on Facebook as far as retargeting goes.

It's not as far as an ad goes but we are going to start dabbling more, I mean I know a lot about Facebook ads, so we're going to start dabbling more on lookalike audiences. My friend David Schloss, I don't know if you know David.

Rich: You know what, I do know David, as a matter of fact I'm just coming out with my product. I'm very happy with Marie by the way.

Karl: Yeah, she's doing a good job with you.

Rich: Yeah, she's doing a great job, look how thin I got; I told her I would lose weight for her. So anyway, we're working on internet marketing together, she's very smart, in fact she's smarter than I am and she's really jumping into the Chris Records, all of his stuff and basically I recommended Chris because like you said, some people when you build a rapport and I have easy access, not that easy because he's a busy guy but to Chris and because he's such a genuine guy and he's a very good teacher, you know you have to pick that one mentor and like you said, you were living in Tahoe at the time, so it was close enough for you to make that commute but there are sometimes where there are people you have to rely on getting a hold on somebody, doing a private message on Facebook or the telephone or they're out on the road and it's awesome to have a mentor to build something like this.

So are you still working with Chris now or are you just actually on your own?

Karl: Yeah I'm pretty much independent now, you've probably seen the buzz but he's building an amazing platform I would say, like a physical platform or school where people can learn these skills and get certified and stuff, so I am actually building like a marketing division for him with that so to an extent I'm kind of working with him but I'm more independent.

I work with people that are launching products; I have a lot of rules for me to help work with someone to launch a product with them that is not always fit. I'm still learning too, I'm learning the brokerage and it's kind of my way to get into the industry, but I also have software and I have stuff I've built in the past and I also have my own products that I'll be launching in the future, so it's just kind of like the steps or the course of steps that worked really well for me.

Everybody is going to be different, I've seen people come out of nowhere and literally blow up in this industry but no one ever sees that backend, no one ever actually sees all the work that they've put in, even like Chris, I know him, I know his background, I've seen why he is who he is, because of his upbringing and because of some of the failures he's had and also some of the successes he's gained. I mean he was really big on another industry before he got into internet marketing and now he's kind of like hybriding the two together.

So it just depends on where you see yourself getting into this industry, if you learn from someone that's been in the industry for a long time and I've seen so many people come and go, rise and fall and so many stay and build amazing platforms, amazing businesses, sustainable businesses, become 8 figure earners in this industry because the opportunity is there, the opportunity is continuing to get better and it's also continuing to get more competitive too, so with that you've to take a little bit with a grain of salt, but Rich, like your platform, you're taking all the knowledge and everything you've learned in all the webinars you've been on, you've probably been on thousands and you're taking that knowledge and you're breaking it down to the simple system that people can follow and I'm big on systems.

So if you use a system or a blueprint that someone can actually come in and actually build their presentation off, build their whole thing off of, it's a win win win even if you don't know what you're doing, you've just got to put yourself out there, 89% or 98% is showing up, right?

Rich: They also say 90% for perspiration, 10% inspiration. You are absolutely right and the key is the structure, the key is the preparation, I think it's preparation meets perspiration.

Whatever the saying is, the bottom line is the 4 hour work week is just a myth. When I say that it's a great book and it was exciting to read, 4 hours a week and I'm going to become a multimillionaire? And for some people maybe they can do that, but we're talking about this industry. Now, take a look at this guy, you know I've got 63 years on this earth and how old are you?

Karl: I'm 39.

Rich: Really? You look pretty good for 39. Chris Record is how old, 29, 30?

Karl: He's like 37 or 38

Rich: Oh my God, I guess it's these old man eyes, but it doesn't matter what age you are. Marie and I were talking about how technology is just improving so much and these 23 years old, I think they had videocon today, that everything is just exploding and how exciting it's going to be and I get to see that my lifetime, but we're talking about- I can hang out with a 23 year old or a 29 year old or a 37 year old and I'm treated like a peer, so there is no real age barrier,

if you have the knowledge then you have the same things in common. Do you not agree with that?

Karl: Absolutely, there's a lot of guys in this industry that are 18 years old, there's a guy that's 17 years old, he just graduated high school and making way more money than his parents are.

Rich: You're right, and it's exciting. So we talked about hosting the webinar, we talked about getting people excited, we talked about having a good product, we talked about the replay and the encore, what do you do about follow up?

And let me throw out a couple of things and I'm going to let you run with it. Do you capture name, address, do you capture phone numbers, do you follow-up by phone, what is it that you do to ensure repeat business?

Karl: So I've never done high ticket, I've only done mid ticket products. So mid ticket meaning like $500 - $1500 and usually with like a 3 pay options, so there's not a lot of phone calling, there might be on a support issue, like someone that owns the product, there could be a phone call that is just to help them use the product, but for us one of our vendors, we've done over a $100,000 with them with the shopified app and it's because we allowed them to turn it into evergreen.

We're dabbling in the evergreen space because-

Rich: Explain it to everybody out there what evergreen is.

Karl: So evergreen is constantly going, it's always open even though it's not live. People have been banner blind, people are educated nowadays, they know that they're watching a replay.

So we do it where they know the evergreen is a replay, but we'll tell them like hey we've got a replay up for a limited amount of days, come watch it. And one of our vendors is actually driving traffic, they're actually driving traffic, they're getting traffic from like YouTube, Facebook and they're doing SEO stuff, they're actually driving organic traffic from people that are interested in that industry, they're actually doing really well and they want a webianr so evergreen is great.

This business can be very spikey; everybody always talks about how spikey this industry is. You have a launch, if it's successful it does multiple six figures and they make a bunch of money, everybody splits up the money, you make maybe $100,000 and you make it fast.

Rich: And that money is spent just as fast as you can make it.

Karl: your girlfriend has a ring on her finger and she's got...

Rich: Well I don't know about that ring on her finger yet but she's talking in $$30,000 ring, so I have to do a really successful webinar. Karl this is a great chat, I so appreciate you coming on and doing this as part of the 50k webinar blueprint, it's an absolute privilege. Before we go ahead and wrap this up, well you mentioned David Schloss, let me just chat with you one quick second about that. Now David Schloss is a guy that basically charges to, he's an expert in the field in driving traffic using Facebook ads and he's very successful in doing that and he does mostly high end spending, when I say high end spending that's $5000 a month that you have to spend on Facebook ads. What do you spend on a Facebook ad in order to make a successful webinar?

Karl: Probably anywhere from 20 bucks a day or so, it kind of depends. I'm doing retargeting ads, I'm not actually doing targeting, but talking about David Schloss he has a system where you need to have a minimum of 10,000 buyers of a certain product in a certain industry and they have to be not 10,000 leads, it's probably more closer to 15,000, 20,000 leads, but you can actually take your leads and upload them into Facebook and Facebook will actually see who they can find on that list and you can actually target those people.

But the secret is and I hope David doesn't get mad at me or anybody else but I've learned this from other people, basically what it does is you can do a lookalike audience and when you have that much data on people, the world is your oyster. So I can go to a guy myself that's in the industry and say like how many leads do you have, do you have 15,000 leads?

Let me rent the information from you or if you have a pixel you can do it with a pixel too, let me rent the pixel from you because pixels only last 180 days, that's the longest they would last on Facebook, but a pixel is kind of like owning an email list but we're just buyers, people are constantly going to come back and be hyperactive with your information.

So then once you have that 10,000 person list on Facebook, Facebook would go out and build this lookalike audience of a million, two million, three million, five million people and they're going to have deep analytics on who those buyers are. It's scientific, it's stuff that I don't even understand, it's scientific so they'll actually go use an algorithm and send my message, my ads, and I can play with different ad variations to see if I can get better conversions coming back to me.

Now that's complicated, that's a lot of stuff, not anybody can just pick up Facebook and know, that's why you have to hire a guy like David Schloss to do something like that for you because that's all he does.

Rich: It's funny that you mentioned that because I'm hiring David Schloss to help me with my webinar business because this is something new to me, and you know what?

Here's another thing too, even though I've been surrounded by a lot of great people and I know a lot of people, I've worked for JVZoo and it's an excellent company to work for, I still don't know enough but I do know that outsourcing is the key, if there is something that you don't know find somebody who does know and either learn from them or scale it up as Chris and Grant and other people would say and take it to that next level, and you know, spending $5000 or $10,000 a month with David Schloss that's going to bring you in $100,000, that's a no brainer. Do you not agree?

Karl: I absolutely agree. That's what he specializes in is loading up webinars from Facebook ads and also high ticket stuff, that's what he specializes in is loading those up for events and stuff like that. I recommend you find out your strengths are and you build off those strengths, things that you're interested in, maybe you're interested in SEO, maybe you're interested in Facebook ads, maybe you're interested in building nice clean websites and funnels, maybe you're interested in doing ecommerce.

You find that thing that you're passionate with and then you do it, that's what you do and you become the specialist, you know what I mean? So David is the specialist for Facebook ads, there's a lot of guys out there, it's not just David, there's a few other people I'm thinking about that actually do the same thing but David is one of the guys- Gary Vaynerchuk his whole business is built off on social media and social media ads

Rich: Now Gary Vaynerchuk is a guy that you know he can't go three words without swearing and yet people love him and I don't understand it. I was in San Diego and all of a sudden people started gathering at the pool because somebody sent out an sms or something that Gary Vaynerchuk was going to be there at the pool, like a rock star throngs of people surrounded him

Karl: I remember EBR said, he posted on Facebook and it was funny because he said let's start a drinking game every time Gary curses.

Rich: Yeah, we have to do it short, EBR is E. Brian Rose who is the founder of JVZoo, he's also my mentor as well as my great friend. Karl thanks very much, it was just an awesome interview. I really and thoroughly enjoy you and I enjoyed talking to you and I also enjoyed the little bit of money that you and Chase sent me today. So webinars are a great thing, I just wanted to thank you very much coming on today and let you know that you are appreciated and I know we're going to run into each other again and I look forward to it.

Karl: Thank you Rich, always a pleasure hanging out with you, the friendship is mutual, everything is completely mutual, and thanks for allowing me to be on here and speak to your people.

Mark Thompson

Rich: Hello everybody, welcome once again to another edition of 50k webinar blueprint, my name is Rich Wilens,. Please welcome all the way from Raleigh, North Carolina Mark Thompson. Welcome Mark.

Mark: Thanks for having me Rich, I appreciate it.

Rich: Thank you very much for doing it. You know, you've been doing webinars for a long time and I remember when you first put together your webinar program, you and I did an interview and I was working as part of webinar swaps and you considered me one of the guys that could perhaps teach some of your students on how to do webinars. How is that going by the way, first of all what is the name of your webinar program and is it still available?

Mark: Yeah, so what we have webinar ignition which is a wordpress plugin that helps you to run webinars through live streaming so you could embed at Google hangout like we're doing or now with other solutions out there now or anything that has a live feed, you can run live and evergreen webinars with that product.

So we have a software component, and I also have a master class, it's a webinar master class where I walk through basically the blueprint of what we do in our business whenever we have a webinar, so how I prepare for it, what are formats are like, how we get people unto the call, our follow-up sequence. So we really walk through A-Z, so have both the software and the training part of it.

Rich: Well, what you've just done is you've asked all the questions that I was going to ask you. Thank you very much for coming by, oh wait a second, I think it's time for you to answer that. So when you're going to do a webinar, do you do a webinar with your own products or are you an affiliate and do webinars with other people's products?

Mark: Well, really both. Certain products align themselves to webinars, I would say, anything that's probably $300 or more it's better to do a live webinar pitch just because when someone is willing to pay hundreds of dollars or thousands of dollars, it's a better marketing outlet to use webinars as opposed to just sending people to a static sales page or a sales page with a VSL on it. It's a bigger buying decision and it's much easier to overcome objections on a webinar format.

Rich: And you're absolutely correct, so it's ok, and I say it's ok if you don't have your product to go ahead and promote on a webinar using your list other people's products because you actually become a partner with whomever it is you have on your program. Correct?

Mark: Yeah, definitely. I would say 50% of our webinars are internal, so maybe it's a product we are just launching or we're doing a test webinar to a segment just to test it out to see how well it converts, and then if it converts well, well then we're going to open it up to our entire list or we'll actually reach out to affiliates and say, "hey, we just did a little test webinar, we'll love to have you run it through your list, this is how it converted." So sometimes we'll just take small segments and do a webinar and then we'll open it up if it's converting well.

Rich: That's pretty awesome. Now, let's talk about the steps that it takes for a webinar to not only start from the beginning but to go ahead and finish it up with a follow-up. So what's the first thing that you do when you produce your own webinar with your own product?

Mark: So the first thing we're going to do is think about what's going to be the big hook, how are we going to get people to attend the webinar. So we'll create a registration page, I'll usually do a video introduction just saying hey, here's why you need to be on this webinar, alright?

Especially, webinars have become so main-stream, people don't attend webinars as much as they used to, one because there's so many webinars out there, and two, they've realized that they get pitched on a webinar, so you can't go into it thinking like you're just going to pitch them, you have to provide some really good training and so you need to have that one, two or three main hooks that people are going to have a reason why they want to attend.

So we try to come up with those few different bullet points and really hammer home, hey this is what you're going to learn, and you have to make sure that you deliver on that during your webinar presentation and then you can pitch them at the end, but if you don't provide that value at the beginning then it can really backfire and you can lose your credibility.

So the first step is creating that registration page, creating that main hook and that's one of the best ways to get people that do register to get them to come on to the live webinar.

Rich: You know I agree with you and I especially agree with you about using the video, people like to see who it is that they're doing business with, and you're exactly right when you talk about what you're going to have to deliver in the webinar.

Since webinar swaps started and all these webinars like you said have been going on for years, people when they put together a webinar all they do is put together either a 60 minute commercial or they know that they're going to get pitched in the end and they wait and wait and wait, and they're just ready for that, when are you going to ask me for some money.

So what you said about delivering content is very good. Now in your video, sales letter in the beginning on the registration page, do you tell them what it is that you're going to present, the type of content, and do you offer any kind of download or cheat sheet or something they can use perhaps to take notes for your webinar?

Mark: Yeah, sometimes. I've learned- if you guys know who Jason Fladlien is, from Rapid Crush, he's another webinar kind of guru that I've really followed and studied, and one the things he always says is, "give them enough that they're enticed but don't give them everything," right? Because you want them to attend, so sometimes what I actually do like an ethical bribe is, "hey, if you attend this webinar live, I'm going to give you X, Y and Z, right? I'll give you a free copy of a piece of software or I'm going to give you this blueprint or mind map, but you can only get it if you come on the call, or hey we're going to give away a free iPad to one lucky person that comes on to the call." Sometimes we'll give little cheat sheets and freebies or sometimes we'll just say, "hey, if you show up live, this is what you're going o get."

Rich: I like the term ethical bribe, I was listening to a Chris Record training program on list building and he says well now it's time to offer an ethical bribe. So not only does ethical bribe work for building your list and capturing your email list but it also works for your registration and to ensure that people are going to show up on your webinar.

Now, in other to ensure people to show up in your webinar there is a certain style or a certain amount of emails you send in other to increase the amount of people who attend. Tell me, what is your strategy to get people to show up to a webinar?

Mark: We usually do three emails. So we usually do one 24 hours before the webinar, then we do one probably 3 hours before the webinar and we'll do one 15 minutes before the webinar. Something else that we've been testing is doing sms or text message notifications as well, so we'll send them if they put in their phone number we'll send them a text message 5-10 minutes before hand, and that's another way to get people unto the call. So we tend not to do more than 3 notifications or emails just because it can be a little overwhelming and people can get turned off from that.

Rich: Well that's a great idea that you're using sms now. Most of the time, when you have an opt-in it's usually first name, last name and then email address, do you find that people are willing to give up their telephone number?

Mark: It depends; it depends on the content, and what type of audience you're catering to. Probably we get 15-20 percent will actually put in their phone number, but even though we would like to get more than that, hey that's 15-20 percent we didn't have before, and once they subscribe you can tell them about other upcoming webinars as well, and you know, it's similar to an email list where they can opt-out to it, so if they want to get those messages they don't have to.

Rich: Right, and I agree with that and the nice thing about getting a telephone number is if they are interested you can almost do a follow-up with that and say, "we have your telephone number"- or not necessarily say we have your telephone number, but you do have access to do follow-up and perhaps close them when they didn't close the first time, so it's an additional. So we're just talking about your email process and you say you do this 3 days, are you saying that when you start your webinar or when you're going to have your webinar, let's say it's on Thursday you go back 3 days prior either Monday or Tuesday and then only send one email, not the second day and then two on the day of?

Mark: It depends. We've tested a few different things, so normally we don't promote a webinar or get people to register until 48-72 hours before the actual live call. We found out that if we start pushing a webinar a week in advance people forget about it, other things happen in their lives, so we don't usually even promote a webinar to get people to register until 2 or 3 days before.

We try to bend the big punch as soon as they register. So they register within the first 2 or 3 days before the call then we would like to hit them with the first reminder usually 24-48 hours before the call and then we would like to have those two reminders really close together, 2 or 3 hours before the call and then one right, hey, we're going live right now, jump on this call.

Rich: Now, in your mailing to your list have you ever used Facebook ads or any kind of SEO to drive people to a webinar registration page?

Mark: Not SEO just because SEO strategy is more long term whereas it's hard to rank a page and drive traffic for a short term event, but we've done cold traffic from Facebook, it works.

We tend to opt people in to a free piece of content and then get them on our list that way and then promote a webinar, but we've run cold traffic and I mean you listen to guys like Frank Kern and Russell Brunson and some of these guys, they throw tons of money at

Facebook ads for cold webinar traffic and they're at least breaking even on it just because they know the value of their offer and how well webinars convert. It does not necessarily need to be hot traffic, it can be cold traffic. So we've done a little bit of it, it's something we would like to scale up though.

Rich: You know it's funny that you mentioned you break even. The whole idea is not necessarily to breakeven but you don't really breakeven when you throw tons of money, it would be great to recoup your investment, but I always thought if you throw a bunch of money out there you're going to get something out there which is that email list, it's that person that's going to opt in. so you're going to have the opportunity not only to make money through that webinar but you're going to be able to keep them on your list and perhaps sell them down the road.

Mark: One of the stats that we always look at is earning per attendee, how much are we making per registrant and people who actually attend the live call, because if that's pretty consistent, if we can say, "hey affiliate, for every person that attends you're going to earn around $15 per attendee," so if they know oh I can get 300 people onto the call then I can make about that much.

Rich: And that's also a way that once you know the number, once you analyze it, it's also a way to scale it up so that you know if you're going to make $15 per hundred, take it to a thousand and you know it just scales up from there.

Mark: Exactly

Rich: So let's talk about the webinar itself. How do you start your webinar and let's say you have your first couple of slides if you do a PowerPoint, if you have your first couple of slides, how do you set people up to let them know that not only are you going to deliver content but there's going to be a pitch at the end?

Mark: Well, the first thing is that we follow a format for almost everything that we do online, like whether it's a video sales letter, whether it's a webinar, we have a 10 step format, and I can actually provide that to your subscribers if they be interested in it, it's a free mind map that we've given out in the past and it works through all of the elements that we use in a sales page, in a webinar presentation, you use the same elements almost in every type of marketing that you do, right?

I mean, introduction, early scarcity, features and benefits, it's a little bit different for webinar because there's the concept portion of it, but when it comes to actually closing and selling them, there is a certain format that we follow, but to answer your question the first thing that we do especially in the first 10 minutes we're really just trying to engage the audience, people come on late, so we want to make sure that we don't really give into the meat of our presentation until about 10-15 minutes into the webinar just to make sure that we max out and get everybody onto the call.

So we usually just remind people, hey turn off all your distractions and tell me where you guys are calling in from, just get people conversing and engaging with you in the beginning just so you can make sure they are attentive before you get into all the content.

Rich: What about the about me page? I had an experience a couple of weeks ago where I joined a webinar and the host introduced the presenter and the presenter went on or 23 minutes telling them all about himself, the picture in front of the airplane and the rose in front of the mansion and where he went on vacation, him and his kids, and 23 minutes before he even got into content at all. What do you feel about that?

Mark: I keep it to just a few minutes max. I mean I think it's important they understand know who you are and why they should be listening to you, so I think you need to give some sort of proof of why they should listen to you. I usually give about a 2-3 minute introduction of who I am with about 5 bullet points just so they have some frame of reference of who I am and why they should listen to what I am saying.

Rich: And that usually takes up the first few minutes and you're absolutely correct. I always preach that you should start your webinar on time, if it's going to be a 7 O'clock eastern time call you start it at 7 O'clock, you can still dance a little bit for the first 10 minutes till more people come in but I always believe that if you start it on time not only it respects the people who are on your webinar and who have attended on time but it also shows that- people always say people don't care how much you know until they know how much you care, so by doing that and starting on time that gives your attendees the respect that they're looking for.

So we've talked about the intro, what do you do in the beginning to promise your attendees that if they stick around, what kind of incentives do you offer? I know you were talking about Jason Fladlien just a minute ago, but what do you do in other to keep the attendees around till they hear your pitch or presentation or your close?

Mark: I reiterate what I say on the registration page, so if we're going to promise something I'm just going to reiterate it and say, well here's what you're going to learn if you stay on the call and then if we have some sort of ethical bribe, "hey stay till the end and I'm going to give you whatever it is," we'll try to tailor the offer to whatever we're presenting. So I just reiterate that from whatever I said on the registration page.

Rich: Some people give away cash and I find that fascinating, stick around we're going to give away five $100 bills, that's enough incentive for me to stick around. You never really know how any people that are going to be on a webinar, there is a maximum of a thousand people on GoToWebinar. What webinar platform do you use, do you use your own webinar ignition or do you ever switch off and use GoTo webinaror webinar jam, and I know they're competitors but I'm just curious, do you always use webinar ignition or do you ever go to GoTo?

Mark: Yeah, we use both. We use GoTowebinar and webinar ignition. So for some of our live calls we use GoTowebinar just because with webinar ignition obviously you have to leverage a live streaming app like hangout, and hangout has a little bit of a delay, there's not as much engagement with the live portion of webinar ignition, so when we do live calls we usually do GoTowebinar.

Whenever we create evergreen funnels where we bring people into an evergreen webinar we use webinar ignition, so it's great for that. I mean we use both; it just depends on what it is we're doing and what type of marketing we're putting together.

Rich: Are you familiar with Amazon s3, do you ever stream from Amazon s3, I know that's pretty popular now?

Mark: Yeah. So a lot of our evergreen webinars are streaming from s3.

Rich: Awesome, and that's something that if you are doing your webinar, if you're on a webinar platform or if you have a plugin like max, s3 and Amazon it might be a little bit reliable than GoTo.

Mark: Yeah, and especially with our webinar ignition platform, we have a custom player, so when it's an evergreen webinar it looks like it's live, we strip out all the controls but you have to stream it from Amazon s3 because if you use YouTube they're going to see the YouTube logo there and they can click it, so that's one of the reasons we use Amazon s3.

Rich: Now, we've gone through the beginning of your webinar, we've gone through your about me page, now we're going into the content. First, let me ask you, how long should a webinar be?

Mark: We generally stick to between 60-90 minutes, we've found that after about 90 minutes, people are busy these days, they have ADD online, they're doing a thousand different things, it's hard enough to keep their attention for more than 30 minutes let alone 90 minutes.

So if you have really good content you can keep them on longer, if your content is so poor then you're going to have to make it a little bit shorter. So we generally try to pitch our; if we're pitching a product, usually between 60, 70, 80 minutes we're pitching that product.

The webinar may extend to 2 hours if there's a lot of engagement and a lot of Q&A that we need to address, but for the most part 60-90 minutes is our sweet spot.

Rich: There's a lot of statistics out there that a person's attention span who is attending a webinar is 51 minutes and that's 51 minutes worth of content, so if you've done your first 10 minutes, whether they stand for 51 minutes or they stand for 61 minutes, I would say that was the sweet spot to go into your presentation. Now, you mentioned you do 60-90 minutes, do you break it down by segments and then stop your segment and then go into a Q&A or a trial close, or do you just go completely through your presentation and then at one particular point you go ok, now it's time for Q&A?

Mark: I would say this, I've definitely picked up a bunch of tips over the years watching guys like Russell Brunson and Jason and you and all the guys that are so great at webinars, I think it's something that no one has ever perfected, you're always trying to tweak and hone your strategy.

One thing that has dramatically increased conversions is after you're done with your content and you're getting ready to pitch your content, you don't just pitch your product and then end it, right? You're always closing, you close 5, 6, sometimes 10 times during that whole closing section.

You may have a hard close in the very beginning when you're presenting, you're stacking your value of what the offer is going to be, then you hit them with the buy link but the very first time you show them the buy link that's just the very first time, right? And then after you've shown them the buy link, then you're going to introduce some fast action bonuses, right?

To help introduce scarcity and get people to take action, right? There's always people that's on the fence, they don't want to pull the trigger, you need to kind of hit those emotional hot buttons and get them to take their credit card out and one of the ways to do that is through scarcity, through bonuses, it's through stacking value, is through close after close after close.

One of the things I did when I first started was my close was about 60 seconds long, now my close is about 20-30 minutes long.

Rich: And you know what? Sometimes you're supposed to, what I like to share with people is to close throughout the entire webinar.

Each different segment is an opportunity for them to shake their head and get them to say yes because when it comes time for you to ask for the money they should be saying yes, and you know of course all closing is overcoming all objections to where people cannot give any reasons not to buy and overcoming objection is very important.

How do you overcome objections and when you do overcome these objections do you know what the objections are going to be and do you address them during your content period?

Mark: Yeah of course, and if you're smart what you do is you take note of the questions that are being asked on your first few webinars. If you're going to keep running this webinar over and over again, take advantage of that and know what the questions are that people are asking and build that into your presentation.

I saw that when Russell Brunson first started promoting click funnels or when he had whatever his webinar pitch was. He had 5, 10, 15 different questions that were already pre-written on slides and he addressed all those, so he was overcoming all those objections and he knew exactly what the main questions were going to be.

So sometimes they were questions that people were asking, other times it was just made up questions to reiterate all of the features and benefits and selling points of his offer.

So of course, if you can, make sure you study and know what those questions are and tweak your presentation accordingly.

Rich: And you know that's a good point too because nobody really knows and especially attendees know that there's a thousand people on the call, there is a maximum number of a thousand people on GoTowebinar, but you can have 50 people on that webinar, you can have 20 people, you can have 200, it doesn't matter.

The point is that when you're doing a webinar people want to know that you're communicating with them, so one of the tips that I tell people is when you're doing a webinar, you're doing this webinar for that one person, that one person that's sitting across from you through the screen and you need to communicate with them, and you have to anticipate what kind of question or what kind of objection are they going to throw up there and it gives you an opportunity to eliminate that, so exactly what you said and I noticed you've been talking about Russell Brunson a lot, and he's one of the guys who has done very well doing webinars with his product and the way he has tweaked that is just amazing, and what I have found Mark, I have done over 400 webinars, over 350 different webinars with different products and everybody has different styles and that's why I look at these styles and I analyze it and break it down, and knowing the objection questions and overcoming the objection questions but making somebody feel like it's that person that's right across from you, that they asked the question and you've answered it to them makes it more likely than not that they'll purchase from you.

Mark: I hundred percent agree. That's what selling is, overcoming objections, right?

Rich: Yeah, and it's closing as well, we always closing but there's also a reason buy and people buy on feelings and they buy on emotions, plus sometimes people have a problem and they need to get that problem solved, but I was talking with somebody the other day and she said to me, "people don't know what their problems are." Have you ever run into that in a webinar?

Mark: Yeah, I mean what I like to do is ask questions in the very beginning of the webinar, so hopefully those questions resonate with the audience, and so when you ask questions that gets people thinking, like "hey, do you have a challenge of XYZ?" and then you're going to give them the solution at the end but the more questions you ask the more participation, and when you ask questions in the beginning you can kind of gauge your audience, say yes in the check box or put a one in the check box if you have the same issues that I do, and if you're getting a lot of people saying no then maybe your marketing strategy is wrong, maybe you're driving the wrong type of people to your webinars, right?

Or, you just need to tweak your presentation to speak to that audience, so you have to understand who your audience is and one of the best ways to do that is by asking questions at the beginning.

Rich: And you know that such a small percentage too of the people who do interact, the people who are going to ask the questions are going to be that select few, there's going to be that 5, 6, maybe 10 questions out of how many people that you have attending; 100, 200, 300, 500, that's why it's always good and I suggest to have those questions prepared, and like you said, once you od these webinars over and over again you're going to be able to know what those objection questions are and you're going to be able to answer them.

Mark: There's nothing worse than doing the webinar, it's going to happen to everybody, right?

Where there are 25 people on and you're like ok, we're going to start taking Q&A now and there are only 25 people, maybe one question comes in and you're like looks like there're no more questions, so that's why it's important that you have questions available, written and scripted out.

Rich: And you know you're bringing up something as well, even if there's 25 people on, and this is how I share with a lot of people who are doing the webinars, whether there are 25 people on, whether there is a hundred people, whether there are 500 people on, I've heard some people say, "well, if you're not going to put a thousand people on a webinar I'm not going to do it," or somebody else would say, "well if you can't get a hundred people on I'm not going to do it," or they get on the webinar and they see that there's only 50 or 60 and they go, you know, I'm not doing this.

But the important thing is that you sent out an email, presenting that this person is going to be on and I'm going to give you information that you need that will help make you do a better webinar and yet they don't understand that whether it's one person or 25 people, these people came to see you and they are potential prospects and they're potential close and they're potential customers life. Do you not agree?

Mark: I hundred percent agree, and one of the biggest piece of this is after your webinar, that is where 50% of your revenue is generated; from the replay.

So just because you only have 25-50 people on the live call, if the follow up sequence is done correctly, that's another 50 people or 100 people or whatever that would see your presentation.

Just because you made X sales on a live call you should be able to double that with a proper follow up sequence.

Rich: You are absolutely correct and it all depends on it's mailed or not. Again, you're just selling another product, you're not selling the live version, you're selling the evergreen or replay, and it's also good for you because if you do such a great webinar for those 25 people, you'll be able to use that webinar over and over again, so there's a benefit for that as well.

Mark: I agree.

Rich: Now, you were talking about once you get to the closing part, so you've gone and you've done all of your content and now you're throwing out the buy link and then you mentioned something about bonuses.

What kind of bonuses do you offer immediately and do you find that most people will buy because of the bonuses and not necessarily because of your product and the content?

Mark: I find that bonuses put people over the edge; it turns a good offer into a great offer and no brainer offer. What we usually do is have one amazing bonus that just kind of blows them away and we make that super exclusive, time sensitive, quantity based, whatever you want, and so we really try to hit that first bonus home really hard.

I would say, "Hey, if you take action right now you guys are going to be able to get this." And then we usually do about 3 bonuses, you know when people start to do 5, 10, 15 bonuses it starts to muddy the offer and it dilutes the value of the offer, you actually think you're stacking more and more value but it makes the offer more confusing to the buyer.

So what we try to do is come up with one or two really great bonuses that are time sensitive bonuses, that are fast action bonuses and then we'll also come up with maybe two or three other bonuses at max, of hey if you didn't get it on the live webinar you can still get these few bonuses to yourself.

Rich: And what kind of bonuses do you offer, do you offer software, do you offer training, do you offer somebody else's product?

Mark: it depends. Again, one thing I learned from Russell was you can only scratch that itch so many times, right?

So you have your core offer which is going to solve one problem, so the bonuses that I always give out are bonuses that can scratch another itch, right? Say someone has a problem with Facebook marketing and your offer has a solution for how you can get more fans or whatever, right?

Well, maybe you come up with a bonus around traffic or around conversion or something complementary to what you're offering, so the last thing that you want to do is give them, if you're giving the core offer which is Facebook training you don't want to give them more Facebook training because your core offer is what scratches that itch.

So it depends on offer or every pitch is a little bit different but, we have a lot of software, so we always try to offer different pieces of software that complement the core offer.

Rich: And I agree with that, so when you have something that people have attended your webinar because they have that particular problem that they feel your webinar or your product is going to overcome, if you offer a bonus that coordinates with this, like you said, if you're doing a program on Facebook and then your Facebook happens to be something to do with content, you can also give them a program about Facebook ads and perhaps how to do Facebook ads.

Mark: Exactly.

Rich: Something that coordinates and makes their bonus just that much more and reason for people to buy. Now you mentioned something about scarcity, do you feel that scarcity is important or is it a sales technique that people are all too familiar with and turns them off?

Mark: It's the number one factor, I think; it's how you get people to buy. I mean if you don't have scarcity people won't buy your product, it's how it is.

I learned that very early on that if you do not offer a legitimate scarcity in your offers of some sort then people will just say oh, I'll wait to buy it, I'll buy it the next day, guess what? They don't do that, so you need to have it.

Rich: You know, people have to buy now because once they leave they leave and you can't rely on them if they're going to watch the replay or not and no matter how many times once they are out of the ether and I call it into the ether, you're exactly correct.

Do you use a timer or how do you offer your scarcity? What do you say to your clients?

Mark: Yeah, we've done all different types of scarcity, the most effective one that we've found is we'll add a countdown timer inside the presentation and we'll do like a 20 minute countdown timer and we'll go through various closes and we'll have kind of like a final countdown timer for 20 minutes and say, "hey, we're going to do some Q&A, we're starting the countdown timer.

Once the countdown timer hits zero then these bonuses will be gone." So we've done it that way, we've also said, "hey, if you purchase on this live call before it ends you'll get these bonuses." We've also done quantity based scarcity where we say, "hey, for the first 25 people you're going to get this bonuses."

So we've done all different types of scarcity and they're all very effective, so I don't know if there's necessarily one or the other, if you do time based or quantity based, but they both are very effective.

Rich: And you know, you mentioned something about quantity based as well. People don't know that you've actually given away 25 and what I suggest to people is you might say there's 10 left, you know what, you can still give away 25 because then again people don't know. I don't believe it's deceptive but I believe it's just a tool that I'm going to give away 10 but I didn't tell them I'm going to give away 10 more and 10 more and 10 more.

Mark: Yeah.

Rich: Do you find that on the replay that if you tell people that the bonuses are no longer available they're not going to purchase?

Mark: Yeah, it's a double edged sword, you've got to be careful with what you promise because you don't want that to bite you in the butt or lose credibility.

If you say, "hey, this bonus is only going to be available on this live call," and people are only watching on the replay and they message your support team and they're like, "hey, I really want the offer but I like the bonuses as well," do you say no, do you stick to your guns or do you open it up?

It's a hard question to answer I should say, so what we try to do, like I said we'll have that 1, 2 bonuses that we save for just a live audience and sometimes we'll just edit the replay and we'll take that part out so they don't even see it.

Rich: Right, and especially if you put it in a strategic place, for the replay you're not going to off. Let's talk about follow-up, on GoTo you have a registration list so to speak and of course usually it's anywhere between 30-50 percent of the people that register will show up, even though you have- let's talk in percentages. You have a hundred people that registered; you have 50 people that show up. Do you use that registration list or do you use just the people who show up or just the people who buy for your follow-up?

Mark: We actually do everybody. Nowadays you'll be lucky to get 20-30 percent on the call, right? If you get a hundred registrants and you're getting 50 people, that's pretty good. Nowadays, it's not like it was 3-5 years ago or 8 years ago whenever webinar started, the attendance rate was 50-70 percent and it just slowly kept going down, right? So you'll be lucky to get 20 or 30 percent. That's why the replay is so important, you need to make sure that you have all of those elements in place; you need to have a good follow-up sequence in place.

We usually will mail everybody who registered, so some people just want to see it again, maybe they just love the content so much, maybe they missed a few pieces of it and they want to go back and watch it again.

So we'll send out a replay for it, we usually send out 3 emails, we'll send out one either the night, like immediately after the webinar, if the webinar did really well on the live call we'll send out the first replay like immediately after.

If it did just ok then we usually send it out the morning; the next day, and then we'll send one out 24 hours after that and then maybe we'll do a final one after that, just depending on how well it converted. If it converted really well we may send out an extra email.

Rich: Well what about evergreen webinars, the recorded webinar, webinar you know is going to be your standard, your basic, your benchmark? Do you use webinar ignition and when you do use webinar ignition do you make it like it's a live event where you have people that are entering the room and some of these names that people are actually getting wise to, or do you eliminate that and just create a presentation that is strictly content and close on a webinar?

Mark: We've done both, if we're going to do an evergreen webinar where it's replay or recording I should say, but we have affiliates that push a lot of traffic, say we want to automate the entire process, we'll actually have somebody that will answer questions in the background, so they can still ask questions and we'll just have someone that mans the chat.

So technically it's live, there's someone there to answer their questions, but the webinar is recorded, and I know plenty of marketers that say, "hey, if I have a webinar that did really well and converted great, I'll use that for live calls, I'll just press the play button and let that run because I know that that webinar converts really well."

Rich: And you know that's a very good tip as well. To have somebody work the backend is very important not only for a live webinar but for a recorded webinar or if you're going to be doing an anchor.

Do you have somebody, when you're giving a presentation is it just you or do you have somebody that can not only answer the questions but to put the buy buttons in, to put the cut and paste or the chat box for them to go ahead and click on it to buy now?

Mark: Yeah, we have someone that mans the chat, they answer the question during the presentation, puts in the buy button when we say the call to action. Sometimes if we're doing quantity based bonuses we'll put in the chat, we'll have them put how many bonuses are left during the close, so yeah it's great to have someone if you can, have someone available to answer questions because, especially if you have a packed house you can't get to all of the questions because if you have 500 or 1000 people on a call it's almost impossible to answer all of their questions live on the call, so if you can have someone answering those questions in the background, at least you're trying to get to everybody.

Rich: You're absolutely right, and plus it shows that you're doing that personal interaction when you're actually typing in and answering the question because now all of a sudden you're putting yourself on a one on one.

They acknowledge there's a human being that are answering these questions and it's more likely than not whether they buy then or they buy in the future, they've all of a sudden built a rapport, and you know everything is relationships and building relationships, whether it's somebody who is just an attendee on the webinar or whether it's somebody who is a prospect who is going to stay a customer.

People buy people, they buy on emotions, they buy on feelings, they buy if they like you, and if they like you they will buy from you and that's a very good tip as well.

Mark: Yeah, well said.

Rich: So let me go ahead and recap what we've talked about today and I'm going to ask you a couple more questions and we're going to go ahead and end this.

We talked about at the beginning of your webinar where you come on and you give them an idea of what's going to happen throughout this entire webinar.

We talked about how long the webinar is going to be; anywhere between 60-90 minutes.

You mentioned that about 10 minutes into the webinar is when you're actually going to start the content but you're going to be building a rapport with the attendees there by talking about not only what they're getting on the webinar but about me page in the story, the hero story.

And then you go into your content. Now we didn't really talk about this but do you segment your content, for example do you 7 minutes one part of the product, 7 minutes on another part, 10 minutes on one part, and then do you stop after each segment to answer questions or do you just do a continuous flow?

Mark: I try to have a continuous flow; I try not to break the flow. What I usually do is build in usually two different spots in the presentation where I'll ask a question and want to get some engagement with them, but the last thing you want to do is get into your rhythm, into your flow and then have to stop and then take questions, because it just breaks everything and you lose kind of your train of thought and the flow of your webinar ends before you know it.

You could have stopped 2 or 3 or 4 different times and then by the time you get to the pitch you're like 2 hours into it and it ruins the whole flow. So I usually try to get some sort of engagement at least two different times during the presentation but it's built in, I know exactly what I'm going to be asking them and then I want them to have a quick answer.

Rich: Now, do you ever qualify your attendees, ask questions, ask qualifying questions as to what it is they're looking for, what kind of problems that they have and then gear that once you start doing your presentations?

Mark: Yeah, and so back to what I was saying a little while ago, in the first 5 minutes I'll ask usually one or two simple questions just to kind of gauge the room and find out a little bit more about who they are, and obviously those questions are going to be related and play into my presentation, but I either want to just get a confirmation from them that yes we're all in the same page here or the audience is a little bit off from what I'm going to be talking about and I can somehow tweak my presentation to speak to that audience.

Rich: And you that's very good because you want to get people to be engaged and a little bit early you said either type in yes or type in the number one because you want people to participate and also it gives the opportunity for whoever that's working your backend to communicated with them and let them know that there is somebody live, there is somebody who cares and is available to answer your questions whether you have one or not.

Mark: Yeah, we usually say in the beginning hey we're definitely going to do a Q&A session but we're going to save that till the end, if you have a question that has to do with the content feel free to throw it up in the chat box, we have someone that's live that will answer your questions but we'll try to address as many or all of the questions at the very end while live on the call.

Rich: And you know, there's one technique that I use that I share with people is that even though you're dealing with somebody in the question box in the backend you always have that one person that says, "well I've got to go to another webinar" or "it's taking too long, I just need to know the buy button or I want to have the buy button." My suggestion is go ahead and give it to them because you're only giving it one person and that's going to give them the opportunity whether they purchase or not.

If somebody wants to leave your webinar and all they want to know is the price it's more likely than not that they're not going to buy then. However, if you can say something like, well give me your email address or you already have their email address because they opted into the webinar, we'll contact you if you have any other questions, knowing that they've got the buy button you can find out if they didn't buy and why they didn't buy, and that's also something that's very important when it comes to analyzing your webinars, don't you agree?

Mark: Yeah, I agree. There're some people that say hey I'm ready to buy now, we demo software a lot during our presentation because we sell a lot of software, so some people as soon as they see the software they're like ok, I'm in, tell me how much it is, give me the buy button, I'm ready to go. So for those people we're not going to like hold them over the calls and have them wait another half hour until we pitch, so we'll give it to them, but yeah sometimes there are people who say, "hey, I've got to go or I've got to go to a meeting or whatever," it just depends on the person, sometimes we'll give them the link or we'll say, "hey, we're going to send out a replay to everybody with a a few hours so you can go and pick up where you left off."

Rich: Right, and like you said, it also gives the opportunity not only to give them the link, but you can also tell them that if you leave this webinar you're not eligible for those bonuses that we offer if you stayed around till the end of the webinar, it also says well maybe I'll stick around.

So that's just the one way you can not only keep them in the webinar but you can keep them engaged.

So we've just talked about the intro, we've talked about the about me, we've talked about the presentation and we've also talked about the amount of time that it takes for the attention span for your webinar.

Now we've come to the close, and you went ahead and you've offered the close and then you've given the scarcity and now it's time for questions and answers. How long do you spend on questions and answers and how do you wrap up your webinar.

Mark: Well, you'll be surprised how many people stay on the call for as long as you want to stay on the call, you can have people stay there for 3 or 4 hours if you keep it going, and that's an opportunity to continue to close them, so the Q&A, I mean we'll have a list of 5, 10, 15 questions that we're going to address regardless of if they're asked just because again we want to hit home all the main points in our offer, but then I usually stay on as long there're questions, I mean if there're lots of questions coming in that means that they are very interested and you need to overcome those objections.

So sometimes Q&A is 15 minutes long, sometimes it's an hour plus, right? So it just depends on your audience, but I'll stay on as long as people are engaged and they'll listen.

Rich: Mark it's totally awesome what we've talked about today, that's pretty much is going to do that but before I go I want to ask, I want to pick your brain a little bit. We've talked about pretty much everything that you do in other to not only make your webinar successful but to help close. What can you offer to the people who are listening or reading the part of this program, what can you offer them; some kind of tip or trick or something that you do that nobody else does or something that everybody else does that's going to help increase closing ratio or increase one more sale or one more conversion or one more follow up to your list?

Mark: Well it's pretty simple, practice makes perfect, right? People are so worried about having everything just right, you have to take imperfect action, so get out there and do your first webinar. Guess what? It's probably not going to be that good, ok? It took me years before I felt comfortable presenting on webinars, so just get out there and do it.

You not necessarily need to have all of the answers, and you'll pick up things along the way. So go and study people who do webinars, get on people's lists and follow them and watch their presentation style, find your own style but analyze the formats, what elements are they putting into their webinars, that's what I did for a very long time.

I was presenting webinars and I wasn't that good at it at the beginning, but I just started watching other people and practice makes perfect and you start to pick up new tips along the way and before you know it, it becomes second nature to you.

Rich: Actually it's perfect practice makes perfect. Mark thank you very much, I mean it's been awesome having you here. Again, you're one of the first people that not only when we did a webinar but using webinar ignition as a blueprint for you- Now webinar ignition, let's talk about that for just one quick second, that's a wordpress plugin, is that correct?

Mark: It is, we're working on version 2.0 actually, I've never actually told anyone that, so this is kind of like an exclusive announcement, but we're right in the middle of development of it, we're turning it into a web app, so it's not going to be a plugin anymore, but the plugin is available for sale but the version 2.0, it's a big project, so unfortunately we're still a few months away before we can even bring on some alpha and beta testers but we have revamped the entire thing and now it's going to be a web app, so you can just use your browser to access the product instead of having to install it on wordpress. The plugin is great, we've been selling it for 3 or 4 years now, so we have tons of thousands of marketers that use it. Great for live webinars, great for evergreen webinars, it has a lot of great flexibility, you can translate it, so if you're on a different language, so it's a great product.

Rich: And where can we get this?

Mark: At webinarignition.com, very easy.

Rich: Webinarignition.com, that's where you can get Mark Thompson's product, it's a great product, I've worked with it, I've known Mark for a long time. Like he said, he's been doing this 3, 4 years and forever in a day. If they wanted to get a hold of you or they wanted to ask you a question, what's a good email address where they can contact you and perhaps pick your brain or become a customer?

Mark: digitalkickstart.com is our brand, it's our company and you can learn everything, all of the different products that we have and then we also have a support desk, so you can just email support@digitalkickstart.com and if you just send in a support ticket, our agents will rout it to me. So that's a great way to get a hold of me or go on Facebook and join our digital kick start Facebook group. We just started it probably about a month ago and there's about 2000 members in there right now but it's very active, a lot of marketers, entrepreneurs, and so you can just search for a digital kick start official group, join that group, and I'm in there all the time, creating new video content and answering questions and interacting with all the members there.

Rich: And it's a great program as well. In the beginning of our hangout today I mentioned you're from Raleigh, North Carolina and there's going to be an event coming up on September and it's an event that we actually met at one of the first times many years ago, probably 4 years ago; Sam England and Brain McLeod's warrior event. There's going to be another warrior even that Sam is doing with Ron Douglas, did you know that?

Mark: I did not know that, is it going to be Raleigh?

Rich: It is going to be in Raleigh and you'll never guess where it's going to be

Rich: Anyway Mark, thank you so very much for spending this hour with us. It was certainly informative, enjoyable, the things that you offered; the tips, the tricks but how you do things are invaluable for anybody who's not only listening to this but who's reading this in the program. So Mark, on behalf of myself I want to thank you very much for taking your time and giving us the information to help make our webinars and 50k webinar blueprint a better product. Thank you so very much.

Mark: It was m pleasure, and it's always good to catch up.

Sean Donahoe

Rich: Hello everybody and welcome to another edition of 50k webinar blueprint, my name is Rich Wilens, thank you very much for joining us tonight. It's an awesome program tonight as we have a very special guest on, his name is Sean Donohoe. Sean has been in the webinar business for many years, in fact he's one of the goto guys when it comes to webinars, doing webinars and most importantly once or twice we were just discussing and he's made over $50,000 in one night on a webinar or so. Please welcome to the program my guest tonight Sean Donohoe. Hi Sean, how are you?

Sean: I'm doing great Rich, how are you doing too?

Rich: You know I'm doing great, thanks for asking. Tonight we're going to be talking about webinars and we're going to be talking about specifically the kind of webinars that you do and I guess I wanted to ask you when did you start doing webinars, how long ago and what made you decide to get into webinars?

Sean: Well, it's a pretty simple background story, I mean we've done a lot of launches, a lot of people know that we've launched a lot of software, we've got our fingers in many pies and many different industries outside of just marketing, but marketing is a very powerful aspect of what we do, obviously it's the fuel, it's the nitrox oxide in everything we do, and a lot of what we've done with launches was great but we saw an opportunity with webinars to condense a lot of what we do and the knowledge and everything else we want to share, message we want to convey and webinars provided that opportunity to deliver that content.

I'm primarily a stage speaker, I speak all over the world on many topics and I'll do these 5000, 10,000, 25,000 dollar boot camps and seminars and everything. There's only so much you can fit into a 90 minute webinar, so what we discovered very early on in the marketing career that I have was we had a really powerful message that we wanted to share with the world, to share with as many people as possible and taking a 3 day workshop and try to deliver that in a 60 or 90minute webinar just wasn't going to happen.

So what we decided to do was take all these $5000 presentations and the knowledge we compressed into that, break it down, record it all, jump in the studio and literally take what we did in these boot camps and seminars, create a $5000 product out of that and then do an introduction, I would say a module one for example and find the best piece of gold knowledge that we could and we put it in a webinar.

Now, I knew nothing about pitching on webinars, pitching from webinars versus on stage, two completely different things, and completely different environments. So I took this one section of our stage presentation and what we were doing in these boot camps and I just taught this one piece and at the end of it we just had a soft pitch that said hey, we've only got so much time here to cover this topic and we're really limited here but if you would like to continue, we've put up this little link or order form, if you would like to get the rest of it.

Now I was planning on packaging this and selling it on the stage anyway, that was my main goal for recording it, but I thought let's just teach it a little bit and see how this works out because I've heard other people doing webinars, doing well in it, I had no idea this time, but that first webinar that we did $75,000 and I kind of just like ok, great.

Here's the thing, I don't have to travel, I don't have to worry about hotel, I don't have to worry about bathroom and everything else and end up in some sort of pitch fest seminar, I just sat down like this in front of goto webinar, delivered an awesome piece of content, sat back, all these sales came flooding in, the email, the replay and I'm like, ok, that was easy, let's do that again and again and it just went on from there, and we refined our process down and everything else and totally really kind of nailed down a solid formula for consistent webinar sales and it's a major part of our income now.

Rich: So let me ask you, how many years ago was it that you did these webinars and how many have you done since then?

Sean: Oh God, hundreds, but I want to say we did our first webinar 2006 and it was a self-hosted, self-created system because like goto webinar it's been around for a long time, actually no I want to say 2007 because it was when I was still doing a lot of ad words and everything else but 2007 I think it was and we were doing a self-hosted video platform, YouTube wasn't really that big a deal then, there was really very few systems, in fact I don't think it was goto webinar, I think it was webex that we were using at the time, and this was really before a lot of the big systems kind of took over and there's a few real big systems and believe me it was a cluster

Rich: exquisite, huh?

Sean: Absolutely, it was a mess, technically it was a mess and there was very few systems out there can really handle the traffic and everything else but we saw the potential there and thankfully we were using all sorts of different systems, we doing very basic PowerPoint, it was ugly, ugly PowerPoint with the voice over and everything else but people loved it, and especially when it came to the replay, I mean most of the sales came from the replays which is just a video in a page and a buy button at the same time and boom, just thousands and thousands of rolling in. so we've done hundreds and hundreds since then. Thankfully bandwidths has increased, technology is so much better, there's so many options out there and you can create extravagant funnels or incredibly simple funnels and deliver that message, get those sales coming, I mean this is the hay days, the perfect time to be focusing on webinars an high ticket sales.

Rich: And you know, webinars are very popular now because of the advent of all these webinar platforms; webinar jam, webinar geo, on24, you mentioned webex, I think webex was one of the first ones that actually gave the opportunity for people to do webinars and live webinars. Now, when you first started doing this it was a PowerPoint presentation, was it not?

Sean: It was yes, and it was ugly, I mean this was before I had any design skills or I had any team really behind me, I'm very fortunate, I married an award winning graphics artist but it was down to PowerPoint, I had no idea really what I was doing but it came down to the message. Now, the presentations we do are a combination of live videos, streaming videos, webcam, we do all kinds of these stuff but you can do just with a basic formatted PowerPoint even now amazing things.

Rich: Now you also mentioned that you would mp4, how do you do that on goto webinar or do you use a different platform when you're presenting a webinar using mp4?

Sean: Well we've got a couple of little tricks, if we're doing a big webinar where we know we're going to be doing that and we're going to be inserting a video, what we do is we'll actually pre- this is a trade secret guys, so don't share this one. So what we'll do is we'll actually sit down and record the entire webinar before the presentation. Now here is the cool thing, you can record an entire webinar, you go through your presentation, recording it gives you the opportunity to edit all your uhms and ahs, restart your presentation if you screw up or anything like that, it's great so that you can end up with a really nice edited piece and if you're doing the live demo, this is a really important thing, a really powerful tip, if you're doing a live demo software, we're software developers, I mean a major part of our marketing business is software development and we have teams of programmers all over the world, one thing that I can guarantee and it's happened to me many times is when we're demoing software live it's going to mess up.

There's going to be internet outage and all that, so we prerecord that session, ok? And then what we can do is we can bring that edit to the recording at the right part and then we end up with an entire mp4, the entire polished presentation, and then another thing that we do is we would actually put a timer at the beginning.

Now, this is a video stream, say it's starting in 60 seconds or 10 minutes or what have you and when we would do that, so the people are rolling in the door, we have little instructions, , grab your coffee, go to the rest room, turn off those distractions and then the presentation starts, on time, it looks professional, it's polished and you look like a rock star, you can even have someone do an introduction and transfer the authority, all the rest of it, but what you're doing is you're playing the video full stream and you're doing what's called a loop back, basically you take a 3.5m jack, another trade secret guys, you plug your output from the speakers into your microphone socket, that way it streams your computer audio through the microphone socket, press the spacebar and your presentation is there live, and then you have someone in the chat box answering questions, you are golden.

Now, that's basically an automated webinar through a live system, however, technology has caught up with us, that's the way we've always done it, webinar jam which is an amazing platform by Mike Filsaime my buddy over there, he created a system where you can do live but you can bring in a YouTube video or an mp4 and then play it and then come back to the live part, all sorts of different options but I just gave you the kind of automated hack for doing alike live presentation and then boom you go.

Rich: And you know you can actually do that too even if you're doing it live, you just have to have two computers and by using that jack you can go from one computer to another and the audio would sound just like it's live and not Memorex.

That's an absolutely great tip that you offered. Now we talked about automated webinars, you like to do live webinars, what is your preference? Do you prefer to do and use goto webinar or do you use Mike Filsaime's webinar jam?

Sean: We actually use both, I actually use about 3 or 4 different platforms, we're always experimenting, click follows for example, webinar geo is the one we've been looking at, using webRTC technology, amazing stuff, zero lag which is important for some of the stuff we do in the stock trading world.

In the marketing world, like IM and affiliate marketing goto webinar, it's funny that people who are very familiar with marketing don't per say trust webinar jam because they know a lot of it is alike live, it's replayed, they have their ever webinar system which is the sister of webinar jam and you can have that webinar going once, twice, three times a day, so it's a replay that looks like a live webinar and everything else.

Outside of the marketing world that system is awesome, it does follow-up emails, follow-up sms and everything else, click funnels, their like live evergreen broadcast, same thing, they can do follow-up sequences, follow-ups to whomever that doesn't attend, sms messages and everything else and that's fantastic for attendance outside of marketing.

Inside marketing goto webinar every time, and if you're going to have a large audience, ask in some of the Facebook groups if anyone wants to sell their grandfathered account because it costs a lot of money per month for one of the thousand unit accounts now.

I was very fortunate to get one of them when they were $79 per thousand and I'm not letting that puppy go.

Rich: And I have the same one too and it was nice because now it's 400 500 dollars. Are you familiar with on24? On24 is a webinar platform that is similar to webinar jam but it doesn't rely on using a hangout.

Sean: That's the weakness of webinar jam, I was going to say that, they rely on hangouts which mean that- and here's the thing, we do a lot in the stock trading world, we're talking about stuff real time happening right now.

If me or one of my coaches is talking about that, we're doing real time stock analysis, we cannot deal with a one minute 20 second lateness. If we're doing anything day trading we're looking at tick per tick on the stock charts, 1:20 can be the difference between a $10,000 and gone, you know, useless for that.

So on24 is great for that and I've looked at that platform a lot. Webinar jam is great, I would say doing a live broadcast and then pushing that to evergreen afterwards then the live doesn't matter, but there is nothing worse than saying ok, do you agree with that statement, put a 1 in the chat box, waiting 1 minute 20 seconds, I've seen it as much as two minutes-

Rich: And you know what? With goto webinar you can have that immediate interaction with the customer, and speaking about goto webinar, how do you feel about working the question box and the chat box? You know as a presenter you're concentrating on putting out the materials and making sure that all of your attendees are getting the information that they've signed up for, do you have any kind of support people that work the question box or the chat box?

Sean: Always. It's essential; I always have one of my senior support staff there answering questions, giving people links, clarifying anything I'm saying because you cannot do it by yourself and you shouldn't.

Remember, the question box is an engagement with your audience, it's where they are, they want to engage with you, they want to ask questions, they want clarifications, those are the prospects you're looking to engage and convert, so it's essential that you have someone there that that can do that.

Now, the alternative is if you're doing the alike live like I said where you've prerecorded everything else, you can then sit in the chat box and engage your audience directly in the background, they can't hear your keyboard, your microphone is off, they're watching the live presentation but you can be there, and now the cool thing is, a lot of people get nervous about broadcasting if they know there's ten people there or a hundred people or a thousand people, right?

Speaking publicly again is one of the biggest fears, so prerecording it allows you to get rid of all that kind of nervousness with the edits but then you can sit there and it's fine to chat with all these people when their questions are coming, which is you can ask for that interaction, bring it in and then play around with it yourself if you don't have someone to sit with you doing it, so that's an option.

Another thing is if you are using webinar jam or ever webinar is if they have a question box and stuff like that that goes to an email, you can sit there in the presentations, have a support member or hire someone from the Philippines, dirt cheap, pennies an hour, that understands what you're doing, can answer most of the common questions, if you don't want them there's lots of options but yes engage with your audience, it's the biggest thing.

I mean this is where I like webinars their own, you can engage with your audience and I love calling out people because I'll have someone flag a question as it goes by, like in goto webinar a little red flag, that way I know that question is relevant, I can a little check there and say ok we've got a question from X and then answer it and my support person once it's answered, bup, goes green and I know that's good and I can keep an eye out because I have multiple monitors and then I can see in real time what's going.

They can't see me, I'm not using a webcam, I've got the presentation and I know the presentation, I'll have my presentation plus the question box and that way it allows me to really talk to my audience, make them part of my presentation, you're entertaining here.

Rich: Yeah, and that's what you should do, remember that person who is engaging with you on the question box they're more likely or not to actually purchase your product, so when you engage with the person in the question box you have an idea of finding out what is his hot button and because you have that person on interaction you have a better opportunity to close them when it comes time as well.

What about collecting phone numbers, a lot of people I know say you know what? If you want to get a hold of me or if there's something we can't discuss or something on the webinar go ahead and leave your telephone number and my staff or one of my staffs or myself will get back to you because we want to make sure that you get the information you need to make the right decision. Have you ever taken phone numbers in the question box?

Sean: Yes, a couple of things we do, talking about phone numbers, phone numbers are very important, there is nothing more engaging than a personal phone call, ok?

We live in this anonymous world of the internet, we sit behind our computers and we have this virtual interaction; put a one in the chat box, that's as far as that engagement often goes.

What we will do is often a times people even though the registration will ask for a phone number, now this is primarily for high ticket sales, I'm talking stuff that's upwards of $2000 mark, upwards of $5000, the reason being we want to make sure that we have an opportunity to close that sale.

So a couple of things that we'll do, first right upfront we'll ask for a phone number before the registration, we make it optional but it allows us to get those sms messages, reminders, get more engagement, remind people that the webinar is coming up because in email we get an average of 147 emails a day, that's the average emails a day for a lot of people, it's easy to get lost in that noise, however, on these we check 97% of text messages that come in, every time it goes off, bum. Get that phone number, it allows you if you're doing high ticket sales to call them up and say hey, with different integrations, with CRMs, you can do hey, did they attend, did they not, order in different sequences, hey noticed you didn't attend, is everything cool, did you miss the replay, etc. or you can have if you have a team like myself, have someone just call them up and say hey, we saw that you didn't attend the webinar or we saw that attended the webinar but you didn't buy, did you have any questions?

And we'll do soft, I hate the hard pitch; the boiler room stuff, don't do that, don't be that person. But if you do a soft pitch for a high ticket product, Russ Ruffino a buddy of mine he's a master of this, did $2.6 million in sales and all they do is a soft pitch, they would do a great value webinar and everything else, drive people through this incredible webinar and then they would mention, they won't even tell you to buy, ok?

They won't even pitch you, tell you a price or anything, he would just say hey if you're interested in learning more click here to set up an appointment to. They don't even talk about that but then they have people on the phone to answer any questions, go over the bits and pieces, what's involved, they're selling 5000, 10,000, 25,000. 50,000 dollar products, this is what we do, it's the same process.

So yeah, if you've got a question what we prefer you do is go and set an appointment, speak to one of our people, that way depending on if it's yourself that's answering it or the support person you've got a lot more control over your time.

If you have a thousand people on a webinar and a hundred people suddenly put their phone number for you to call them, that's a mess.

You're going to end up all over the place, you're never going to have time to do that, however, for the people who are really interested it acts as a self-filtering process, by then going on a booking system, you can get like bookly or all sorts of other systems and have them set an appointment, and then you can schedule your time and they can see when you're available and they're expectant of that phone call, they know there's going to be someone there, you have the time organized to speak with them or your team does, boom! Absolute gold.

Rich: And you know that's a big thing that's going on now is people are taking applications, they're not mentioning the buy button or exactly how much it costs and they're taking phone numbers as well because who better to close when you have a thousand people on a webinar or 800 or however many it is but yet that person who does give you that phone number all they're looking for is validation and they're asking for the information that you can deliver to them in order for them to make the right decision and that's the only thing they really want to know is they need that confirmation that they are making the right decision and by getting a phone number or taking an application, you know, everybody seems to be doing it now and I think that's the right way especially in a high ticket item the way it's going. I know you agree with that.

Sean: Absolutely, and one thing I would say there is if someone is committing to a call and they're wanting more information they've already self-selected themselves, they want your product, ok?

What they're looking for kind of like what you are say is validation, but they want to talk to someone to make sure that any objections in their head are cancelled so that they can proceed, and this entire application process which is another alternative way is a great way because they self-answer and sell themselves.

With the application process one thing I always do and it's kind of a role reversal is why should we accept you into our program? And what they're going to do there is they're going to answer that one question to convince you why you should let them in, and by doing that they're selling themselves, and if you say ok, well we saw this answer and this is why you want to be in, great.

What can we do here to make sure proceed? Now they've already self-selected, they don't want to back down from that, it's a great closing technique.

Rich: Exactly right. You know, everything is overcoming objections and the reason people don't buy is because you have satisfied by giving them the information they need, so that's what you need to exhaust all the objection either before they come up or after they come up and what better way not only to address the objections to a phone call, but through that application process they will tell you how you can close them, you know, you can't sell them and not close them.

I know a lot of people who would do a webinar and they're great at selling and they give all the information they need and they get people to say yes, they get them to agree but they don't ask for the sale or they ask it poorly. So you're absolutely corrects and it's such a good way to not only overcome the objections but your customer will tell you how to close them, and that's an important tool.

You have a bunch of tools that I noticed on the last webinar that we did specifically on goto webinar, when we were doing our goto webinar you had a separate link, once they registered it went right to your link where you did a video and I think you gave away a pdf. Can you explain a little bit about that?

Sean: Ok, we have several different technologies that we use, we're always developing new ways, so what we do- we have a product coming up for example called Leads Flow Pro, its launching on July 19th, not a pitch just telling you why. What this system will do is it will allow one click registrations to goto webinar which we cannot do normally. So rather than just going to a signup page and everything else, it's a pain in the butt, you always have drop off say between email blast and then they get to goto webinar then you've got about if you're lucky 30-40 percent uptake on that which means you've lost 60-70 percent of your leads.

So what we do is we have a link that goes in your email that instantly registers them, but they also can instantly put them on your auto responder, instantly send them an sms, save and push notices, all sorts of really cool technology that we do. So what happens then is this one link stays throughout the campaign, now it's a very powerful thing that we've recently added this.

So with the lead flow where you have this one click registration, when it comes time… we may also deliver a lead magnet, we'll say hey, when you sign up you'll also get this free guide or this primer piece that lays the foundation for the webinar and that's very powerful indeed because it sets the tone for the value they're going to get, they know the topic you're going to talk about, you've created this teasel of presell for the content itself framing the value and when you deliver on that value you create massive reciprocity.

So this one link does all of that; signs them up, sends them an sms, gets them on your auto responder which you can't do with goto webinar, you don't have any chance unless you're doing all kinds of [systems, and then we deliver that lead magnet, we've got all these other integrations now.

On the day of the webinar what we do is we then send them right to the goto webinar link, everything else is gone, we want them right there at the time of the webinar, then as soon as the webinar is over we change the redirect in this lead flow to a replay coming soon and again we'll include the link to the download of the free guides so that anyone who is following any of your older emails, maybe they've gone when it was 3 days ago they're still clicking on that link, they're not just logged into a webinar over, like page from goto webinar or any of these default pages, that would be a lost bounced lead which could be a sale, but if they know hey, replay coming soon, here's some value or ok and then you put the replay up, you change the link in your lead flow, and then what happens is anyone is clicking in caller broadcast for your replay, old emails for hey coming soon or your broadcast is about to start or hey this is happening tonight and everything else, any of the old emails in the sequence or any of the promo which we found can give you up to 15-16 percent extra set of leads and clicks not to be ignored when you're converting 1000, 2000 dollar product.

They continue through the flow and it's all the same link throughout your campaign, amazing results.

Rich: Will this link work on doing Facebook ads or somebody clicks on a Facebook ad?

Sean: Absolutely, here is the cool thing, say we use A webinar as an example, this link would be say yoursite.com/rich and then it's got email equals X, first name equals X, last name equals X.

Goto webinar for example requires 3 parameters, those three. If for example one of those links doesn't exist like the email or the first name or you haven't collected those pieces of information you can default back to a registration page.

In other words, some of those parameters don't exist to alter register them, we still have a fall back sign up page.

That would work as well with Facebook, so Facebook ad, banner ad, video ad or what have you signup, but you're going to have the email, you're not going to have the first name or last name but you can push them through to the flow so to speak and it still ends up on their signup page, so it works regardless.

However, with leads flow pro we also have the support for Facebook lead ads which you can create lead ads which have their name, email and everything else prefilled, they click a button and boom!

One click, auto registration from Facebook lead backs. So there's lots of different ways you can use this technology to do that and have a lot of fun on streamlining your webinar process, I'm not saying this to pitch leads flow pro, what I'm saying is we've run our biz on this for the last year, we built it for ourselves for the single purpose of maximizing our webinars as well as every other aspect of our business and affiliate and promotions and marketing campaigns, and that's what we built it for, to streamline and optimize our webinar processes specifically.

It's a wordpress plugin, it's a very powerful piece of kit, it's not just a webinar system, we call it the lord of the rings, it is one system to rule them all. It integrates with everything you do, all sorts of different SAS platforms, auto responders, webinar systems, membership systems, CRMs, basically you get one lead and you can trigger a whole series of events, track what your leads are doing, see what they are interested in, build real intelligence about your audience, see who is buying what, it's literally an all in one system for marketing automation, it's a very cool piece of kit, we built it primarily for ourselves, we've been using it the last year in most of our business now and yeah, it's been brilliant for us using this and integrating with specifically webinar jam, goto webinar, we also support webinar ignition from Mark Thompson and even support for webinar geo and lots of other platforms as well.

Rich: Very good. Let's talk about webinars for a second, I know you host your own webinars but what about affiliate marketing, do you host other people's webinars and mail to your list and how well have you done with other people's webinars on your list?

Sean: Very well. Now to me it's a great partnership because all you do is- I did one recently, funny story and I won't mention names, did a webinar recently with a guy who was in Bali, there were two presenters, one in Bali which is in Indonesia, one in Hawaii, very time zones.

Now the guy in Bali couldn't get on goto webinar, bad connection, so he was doing it on his phone speaking but he couldn't bring up the webinar presentation, ok? So he emailed the presentation literally before we went live to the guy in Hawaii who was actually broadcasting it.

So we've got one guy speaking in Bali just on his phone presenting, couldn't see the presentation but he knows it so well in his head. The other guy is showing the actual screen, they're going through it, the webinar went on for three and a half hours, it was an amazing content and everything else, and I'm thinking Oh my God this is a complete mess, this is not going to do anything, I'm here I've got to do it, you've got to get to the end of the show, and at the end of it I'm like passing out like ok this is an endurance marathon, it is still one of the best damn webinars I have ever done in terms of conversions, it was amazing conversions, I'm like ok I'm not going to make a single sale, everyone is kind of laying faced down on their keyboards, it's done.

But conversions kept coming in, replays were amazing, so yes, doing other people's webinars, sometimes you scratch your head at some of the webinars and the webinars that are out there but if they've got good dynamics, if they've got a good personality, if they've got a good product which is obviously important and they've got a service staff that can back up their claims then yes it's a no brainer because all we're doing is mailing out a few swipes here and there getting people signed up, getting them on the webinar, boom!

Done deal, an hour later you've just made $100,000. Someone else is doing all the hard works, the delivery of product; you walk away with a smile on your face from here to there and waiting for the cash to come in, it's great.

Rich: You know, let's talk about structure on a webinar for a little bit, how long do you think a webinar should last before you actually go into the pitch? They say that most people's attention span is 51 minutes, so you go into a webinar; I know were talking about some people having a 3 hour webinar, what is a good time, what do you suggest is the right amount of time when you should go into your sales page and your sales pitch?

Sean: You know that's a good question. It depends on the industry, you've got to get a sense of your audience, every audience is different. If you've got a new marketer audience, less experienced, their attention span is much shorter, if you have a high dollar audience for example what we do in the stock market world, we've got people that have a lot more disposable income, they've got a lot more focus on value, content and results, they're going to have a higher tolerance full length.

A lot of people have said 60 minute and then get to your pitch, ok? I hate that, the reason being I want to connect with the audience on three levels; I want them to be engaged, I want them to be entertained, enthralled and even if they don't buy I want them to walk away feeling, damn that was awesome, and the thing is a lot of strategies you can barely scratch the surface, if you're giving really good value content I think it takes a little longer, I usually try to keep my entire webinar to about 90 minutes. So just after the hour, usually I like about a 15-20 minute close, but it depends on the audience. If I'm like talking to someone who is very engaged as the co-host or host of the webinar there is going to be back and forth and bant of more conversation which is more entertaining, it keeps your audience more engaged, they feel more charged.

So I think that can really have a big difference, yeah I've had webinars that go for 2 hours, so if I'm doing for about an hour and fifteen to about the 90 minute mark and then get to the pitch, that's fine, it can go on.

You've got know from your audience what their level is, you'll see it by their questions, the comments, the engagement factors, if it's starting to drop off then you know your presentation is too long.

I am known for longer webinars, about 1 hour 30 minutes to 2 hours, but I always like to give so much more and make sure that even if- you're only going to close 10 to 15 or maybe 20 percent if you're really good, 80% of the people who are there, who have invested their time in you, what you have to share and f you're not delivering really great content or strategies that your customers can use or the host customers can use then you're doing them a disservice.

If you want to bond and brand yourself as well give massive value, over deliver value, stand out from the crowd, go way above and beyond what other people do because a lot of people are there for oh, three steps, buy my product, and it's minimal content, and you feel like you've been violated.

Over deliver, give away your golden information, make people go damn! Get them glued to the screen with the value give and the presentation and you'll have sales no matter what you're offering.

Rich: You know, I agree with that and I was a strong believer, I said if you're going to go ahead and make a presentation you're never going to be able to give all of the product and all of the information that you normally would give when you deliver your product, but if you do take those three 15 minute segments, let's say 45 minutes and you deliver your best stuff people will realize that you are just giving them a value.

You mentioned the term "over deliver", I like that term but I like to say that people who go beyond expectations and who justify not only the products and the information that they deliver, but you're absolutely right, they close more sales and 10 15 20 percent, that's an awesome sales closing ratio when it comes to penciling out the numbers.

I mean if you take 100 people and you can sell 10, you know if your price point is 995 and you're selling 10 and 100 people show up, that's $10,000 and of course scaling it up, if you bring 1000 people it's $100,000.

So I see exactly where it is you're coming from. Let's talk about for a minute, you have a beginning, usually it's an intro whether you're working with a host or not, and then you go into what I call the hero story, the rags to riches, the guy who went from delivering newspapers to being the webinar king.

How long do you think a hero story should go and do you really think that if they go on for 10-15 minutes it helps or it hurts the presentation?

Sean: I skip it, I skip it altogether, I cut it out of my presentation. Here's the thing, no one gives a rat ass about you, who you are, your background story or anything like that, ok? If you're going to do a brief introduction about yourself give a little bit of your authority, background or why they should listen to you.

I stole this from Collin Theriot: four questions you should ask or answer for your customer; why me, why you, why this, why now?

The why me is why should I care about what you have to say, why should I waste my time or invest my time in why you have to say, why is it relevant to me, what I'm I going to get?

We are all very self-centered creatures and again in the marketing world especially people are about webinars, you're seeing the attendance number drop off, you see the engagement drop off, seeing very aggressive questions; what's this all about, what's the price, what's the pitch and everything else and people are kind of getting very skeptical or hostile, so this is what I say and this is the way I like to approach a lot of my webinars.

I tell them what they're going to get, who it's for, why they should stay tuned in all the way through and what they're going to get at the end, ok?

Now that addresses the why me. Now the why you should be very brief, lay your authority down, what you've done, you've had a transfer of authority from hopefully the host or if you're doing it yourself.

If you've got a transfer of authority they should have already have a bio in the introduction that's just brought them to you and that should be enough, you want to get right into the content, the value and everything else as soon as possible.

No one cares about the one legend golfer in terms of webinars.

Stories are useful, an for the point you're making.

If you're a one legged golfer with a perfect swing no one wants know all that, they don't really care, they want to know what is in it for them, not altruistic but self-centered but it's the way the world is.

You've got address those skeptical buttons right off the bat to get them to say- basically break out the noise. If everyone is doing X do Y, stand out because there's a lot of noise that we're folded with, everyone is snap chatting with 6 seconds of pocket links attention span, again your audience is going to be the same.

Break the cycle, pattern break all the way through, shock them with the value you're going to give them, spend about 5 minutes telling them what they can get and then get right to the point, get right to the value of the content and you're going to have that attention all the way through.

If you've got a story that's relative to your content, deliver that, that's fine. In one of my webinars I talk about when I was working in New York and I talk about a deli and a pizza joint that was around the corner, the deli closed like peak lunch time.

So there was a deli around the corner that got my attention and I have a big story about that because it's relevant to the point I'm making about the right message, the right person at the right time. So dropping stories in perfect, but your entire life story? No one gives a rat ass.

Rich: I agree with you and I remember one time somebody emailed me and said they attended a webinar and the first 23 minutes was all about them and then they did about 10 minutes worth of content and it's all a waste of time and they just got very discouraged about that, so I do agree with you about that. So when you're doing a webinar and you know you want to start closing and usually I suggest to people that they should start closing just from the minute they say hello, getting people to say yes throughout the entire webinar which includes asking open ended questions and questions that you know that are going to be objections in overcoming them. Do you have questions prepared knowing that people who are on your webinar are going to ask these questions and then do you overcome the objections and get people to say yes throughout your entire webinar?

Sean: Absolutely. One of the things that we did in the webinar we did recently; you and I, one thing I like to do is… very common in this industry you say put 1 for yes 2 for no, one thing I like to do is I say type in yes if that makes sense.

The reason being I want them to actually type the words yes, very powerful sales psychology technique that we do very much in our high ticket webinars, because the more they're saying yes to pre-framed questions and statements, you're creating a symbiosis between you, your message and where their mind is thinking, understand your audience, their common pain points, the ways they're thinking, the objections they're going to have; oh is this going to be too expensive, oh is this really going to help me, is this same as every other system I've seen in this industry?

If you're answering this, first you want to separate yourself from everyone else, you don't want to be a salesman you want to be a guide and if you're guiding people rather than selling them they're going to be right there with you all the way and you keep pre-framing your close, pre-framing your conclusions with statements and questions you know they're going to agree with then again you've got them on the yes path, so all the way to the end when you start saying ok, this is very important, when you're going from your content to your pitch starting with transition, you're seeding your end always in mind. I always start my webinar saying hey we're going to deliver awesome value, at the send I'm going to show you how we can continue this training and everything we've been talking about because we've only got limited time here today.

What you're doing by doing that will right upfront is saying we're going to deliver some great value but there's not going to be enough time here, I would like to continue.

You've already got them agreeing to that and saying hey, is it ok if I show you how we can continue this at the end? Yes.

Rich: Yes, and you know a bi-product of having them type in the yes is you're telling them what to do and when it comes time for you to close the sale what you say is ok go ahead and type in yes on the buy button and go ahead and take advantage of this wonderful offer, so that's where the psychology come in, it's all about the psychology and getting people to say yes and telling them what to do because that's what they want, they want an authority figure to tell them what to do and if you combine that with the information that they need to satisfy their pain point, to give them a reason to purchase, that's going to solve a problem for them and that they're going to benefit from it.

You know whats said is absolutely correct, it's when, where and why and why am I here and is this going to benefit me?

So I totally agree with all the concepts that you talk about. I want to talk a minute about follow-up, what do you do about replays and what do you do about encore performances? Is it effective for you whether you mail your own list or you mail somebody else's webinar that you hosted, is it effective for you to do a replay?

Sean: Yes, absolutely. Now encore performances are not as effective as they used to be. What it used to be was we'll do a webinar and then two days later we'll have oh did you miss this one? And then we'll have an encore which is basically a replay, broadcast, like live through goto webinar or what have you at a slightly different time zone, that way you're catching different people at different times, and it's become less and less effective, so what we'll do is simple; webinar and then a 3 day replay sequence, and what we're doing is we might have day 1 standard replay, day 2 we might introduce a payment plan or payment option. One thing that's working very well right now is the interest free payments.

Rich: 6 months interest free.

Sean: Yeah, so if you are doing something like PayPal as an option you can pitch that as a payment plan, you get the money immediately, full amount, you're not waiting on rebills and expecting them to drop off and cancel or something like that but they still want your awesome training or whatever you're doing, but if you offer 6 months interest free credit and say hey, you might have this option in your country and so on, obviously make sure you have that option with your payment process, I think JVZoo if you're going through checkout you can still get that option and stuff like that as an example, clickbank definitely does with their integration with PayPal, so a lot of different options there.

So day 1 is straight replay, day 2 offer a payment option or something extra, maybe scarcity, extra bonus hat everyone gets who buys right now and then day 3 is the closing email sequence, we'll send out 3 emails; one in the morning, one in the afternoon, one in the evening with a timer; email timer or something like that, we use mail timer pro which is available for free, it's one of our free products and again timer on the replay page, it's counting down and then do yourselves a favor guys, if you say you're closing it at midnight close at midnight. So many people would say oh I might catch those one or two extra sales, yes but you're showing your audience you're a liar, you're not genuine. So closing it down at midnight trains your audience, so if you say it's closing, it's closing.

Rich: Right and you know what? You also have to start your webinar on time, how many times have you been on a webinar where people, let's say it's 8 O'clock and the host would say you know what? We don't really have enough people, we're going to wait another 10 minutes so we can get a bunch of other people. You know, that's absolutely wrong, if you're going to say it's an 8 O'clock webinar you must start on time always, otherwise what about the people that are already there? I think it disrespects them and it puts a sour taste in their mouth.

Sean: Very disrespectful indeed and yeah, I've even had it where the... I've got to be careful what I say but I've had people who have a really great presentation, everything is cool, everything looks like it's going to be great and then they bail on the presentation or you've not go enough people there.

Look, attendance records are through the floor, you've got to be innovative, you've got to do all sorts of things to get a higher and higher audience or attendees but listen, at the end of the day most of the money now is in the replays.

Rich: Right and you know what else?

When people show up and there's only 20 or 30 people, and I hear this a lot, I'm not going to do the webinar because there's only so many people.

You know, those 20 people were interested enough in that promotion, that email, however they got onto that seminar to come and see you, that's 20 prospects that you have that you might as well deliver. I always believe if you have one prospect or if you have a hundred or if you have a thousand always deliver your best because those are your customers.

They might not buy today but if they know that you have delivered your best material and your content they will eventually buy down the road, do you not agree?

Sean: I agree with that 100% and the flip side of it is if you're hosting someone else's webinar be upfront with the presenter of how many people you can bring to a webinar.

If you can only bring 50 people to a webinar say that. Here's the thing, I can only get about 50 people on the webinar but will mail the replay, will focus on that, we'll make sure it's all cool and that way you've got a true relationship.

So if you've got someone that says if you're only bringing 50 people I'm not doing it, well guess what? Move on, find someone else, there are plenty of other people you can do business with that have integrity and won't mess up your business because there's nothing that makes you look bad as the host of someone else's webinar than having your audience turn up and the person is not there.

Now, check your time zones because I've screwed this up before because I moved from California to Texas where I said one time zone like PST which is what I used to be and I meant EST. so I had it once when I had a webinar that started 3 hours early and I had people there, and the webinar presenter was like I'm not going to be there for another 3 hours and you're going what? So I've actually filled full of content for 3 hours before the webinar started, that's why I'm the only person I've ever heard that's done that, so yeah, make sure you read time zones as well.

Rich: Yes, I did that once when we had webinar swaps, I started an hour early and the presenter wasn't supposed to be there for another hour so, I outlived, which by the way, a funny story that you and I had, I like doing a pre-show, when I was working and I still am working for JVZoo and still doing the JVZoo webinars I usually do a pre-show because what that does is it gets me to interact with the audience and get some warmed up. Joel Comm likes to come on 5 minutes before and goes hey, how are you doing and where are you from and all that whereas I like to deliver with the people that are coming onto the webinar to build their trust because I believe as the host I have an opportunity to close my list as well because who would be better to help close is the person who is the host and it's his list that he mailed.

So I believe that when you do a pre-show you get people all warmed up, you get them ready to go, you build that rapport and when it comes time to close they're going to listen to you because they've already had that rapport. Now, with that being said I've always started 15 minutes 20 minutes early but when it comes time to start the webinar and if it's an 8 O'clock or 7 O'clock we always start on time.

Sean: Absolutely.

Rich: And I believe that by having that pre-show like I said it just builds the rapport with your customers. Sean it's an excellent interview that we had, let me just ask you one thing before we just kind of wrap this up.

What is one tip, one secret or something that you could suggest to the people who are either reading this or watching this, something that has helped you make more money with webinars?

Sean: That's a good question. Know your numbers, it's the most important thing you can do with your webinar.

Rich: Are you talking about closing numbers and ratios?

Sean: I'm talking about all the numbers involved in the entire equation. Know your conversions, your average conversion on a webinar.

Now, if you're doing affiliate webinars, if you know that you get a hundred people you close an average of about 10%, you know that if they've got about a thousand registrations about 30% of people may turn up, that's kind of all of them.

Ok, do you get a thousand registrations you know about 300 people are going to turn up depending on the engagement, the list and everything else, closing 10% of sales on average, you can start kind of factoring and you get 30 sales which means you know your numbers.

Now if you're doing paid promotions, what's your cost per acquisition per lead? If you're doing say $4 per registrant, you know if your numbers hold true, you'll know this as you go forward, if you're doing $4 per registrant and your product is worth $1000, ok?

So if you that for $4000 you've got a thousand registrants, 30% of people turn up you know ok, 1000 registrants, 300 people turn up, 30 sales and $30,000, let's keep it simple numbers, and if you've invested $4000 and you've got $30,000, guess what?-

Rich: $26,000

Sean: Another example is if you're doing a $5000 product, doing a high ticket thing, you know that it's going to cost about $1000 a sale, we're talking really high ticket stuff here obviously; $5000 $10,000 stuff, but if you know you can spend $1000 to acquire a sale, like most people thing $1000 for a conversion? Oh my God, I'll never do that. Scale it back, if it's costing you $100 to make a $500 sale or $10 to make a $50 sale, that's a bloody blank check but you'll never know that if you don't know your numbers, if you're not too sure about your conversion statistics, you're not too sure about your engagement, how your offer is converting, you're not slip testing your registration page, slip testing your ads, there's lots of different ways.

We're focusing a lot more these days obviously for a paid traffic as you can probably tell from what I'm talking about, that's huge for us, Facebook traffic, YouTube ads, ad words, all the different networks, we're focusing primarily on Facebook, but if you know your numbers it gives you the opportunity to do so much more, there's no such thing as a traffic problem, there's no such people as a lack of people to view your content, it's all in the conversions so you're just going to make it happen. So know your numbers.

Rich: And that's what I was going to ask you, how effective are Facebook ads or Google ad words or doing YouTube traffic, you talked about $4 to get somebody in, you know you're absolutely right, it's all based on the numbers, but tell me how does Facebook ads work for you and how much do you spend let's say on your $497 webinar, how much would you spend on Facebook ads?

Sean: You know what, rather than talk about that campaign let me tell you one we're running right now. We're running a very powerful campaign with a $20,000 ad spent, our way on that is insane on that is insane. It's very difficult to say because I don't want to give away too many of my internal secrets so to speak, but let's just say scale up slowly and we would blow up a lot of money, and here's the thing, a lot of people say well put them on a link magnet and then offer them a webinar.

Forget that, go straight for the registration, for the training, tell them what they're going to get in the ads, the benefits, why me, get them on that registration, reinforce that benefit and what they're going to get, the results and everything else, get that registration, follow up with the reminders, follow up with the replays and everything else, maximize your conversions there, make sure you know everything that's going on and it doesn't matter how much your cost per acquisition is, as long as you're making more money than you're paying.

The thing is we run different campaigns for different things all the time, we're always experimenting, last couple of weeks Facebook has been making some big changes which has pushed our cost per acquisition up to $10, but if we're making double our money back, ok cool, fine. We just keep refining, keep changing, with Facebook we're most focused on a $1000 plus, so we change our offers around, we add more here, change a few things until we're happy with it because we've got to make sure we're getting more out than we're putting it, so one thing that- and this is another great tip a well, have an upsell with your webinar.

How may webinars have you gone to and it's one product and it's like a big no no for webinars is don't do upsell, why not? If you can get another 30% or even if it's another 15% on a high ticket upsell or pro-sell or something like that, it's a no brainer, it's extra money for you, your business and you're doing your customers if you're giving them more value, an opportunity to invest more because they're really open to you, what you have to offer, that's more money for you, it's more benefit for them, why the heck not? And you can add a massive amount of extra profit from that which will more than cover any ad spent, even if you're breaking them on your webinar just as a kind of scale thing, that's extra 15% bonus is gravy.

Rich: I agree with that and you know sometimes I've seen where people offer an alternative of choice and when I say that when people go in and they give their pitch for the webinar they usually give one price and sometimes they would split up the payments, but if you've got like you said an upsell you can give them what I call is the alternative of choice where you have three buy buttons offering three different products and instead of just giving them the opportunity to say no you give them the opportunity to either pick one, and no matter what it is you will at least get a sale in and I believe that it does increase your conversions. Do you agree?

Sean: We've tried that and we've found it to be the opposite because you're giving too many options, you'll end up with a confused audience because they're like ok, so what was it from this one? Ok we've got this this this, we've got this this this and it kind of creates confusion.

For us and this is purely our data and everything else we found that giving them one option to proceed has been best. Ok this is what he says we're going to get, we don't have to think about it, we're already programmed psychologically, this is the power of the pitch, it's got us to this point, we have that one decision to make; yes or no and if no, why not? Adding two options like payment plan we found that since we offer a payment plan everyone goes for the payment plan, we would like that large chunk upfront, and a lot of people have done well this is the pro plan, this is the go plan, this is the basic plan and depending on your product obviously and your pitch.

You can get much people on the top level and providing all those other options is great to down sell themselves but with webinars we've found that people are so engaged and then too many options is like slamming on the brakes, you know you are in a Ferrari, you've got the pitch, you've got the pace through all the value of the content, through the transition, through your close, your multiple closes and it's like they're shifting gears, they're in the Ferrari going down the highway 180m/h and then there are three choices, it's like three on the road and they're like oh crap! So for us we like to take off the exits, keep them on straight and boom all the way to the finish line.

Rich: That's awesome Sean, thank you so much for sitting in with us tonight and I know you're a very busy guy, I do appreciate it. Thanks for coming on, the tips that you've given, you've delivered beyond expectations and I just want to say thanks once again very much.

Sean: My pleasure, glad we could have a chat.

John S. Rhodes

Rich: Hello everybody and welcome to another edition, one more edition of 50k webinar blueprint, I'm Rich Wilens just in case you didn't know that, you're not but I am and what the heck. I'm so happy to have a special guest on today, I've known this man for quite a few years, he excels in the field of webinars, his mind is sharp, I've seen him in many events plus we've had him as a guest on webinar swaps and JVZoo webinars, so let's just go ahead and jump right into our 50k webinar blueprint. Please welcome to the show today my friend John S. Rhodes, hello John S. Rhodes.

John: Hey Rich, how are you doing?

Rich: Hey, I'm doing great actually. Thanks very much for taking your time, I know how busy you are and I do appreciate it. The program is all about how to make $50,000 on one webinar and I know it can be done because you've done, the people who I've interviewed have done it, we've done it o JVZoo webinars as well as webinar swaps. What I like to talk about today is I would like to talk about webinars. First of all, what is your background in internet marketing and when did you get started in webinars.

John: Oh yeah, so it actually goes back to the late 90s when I was actually using some technology in the corporate world and also in some my consulting and it was with Citirx which is the mother company of goto webinar and goto meeting, and I actually got started, I wasn't making money then, I was working for the man at that point in time but I got introduced to webinars, I got introduced to these online meetings and sharing, it was all the rage to be talking about telecommuting, how you're going to have all these virtual offices around the world, this is before the internet really was taken off in the late 90s, it was like just starting to really take hold, and so that was when I was first introduced to webinars at all and it kind of got the gears turning.

At that point in time again I was working for the man, I was in corporate America and I started to realize and started to understand that this was not only an effective training platform because that's really how Citrix and goto webinar and then obviously these other platforms started out, they were really all about training and educating, they were not about selling at that point in time, and no one really made the connection that they needed to make early on, no one made the connection between the ability to broadcast and to almost be on stage in a virtual sense using these webinars.

People were still back in the late 90s and early 2000, they were very much doing teleconferences but without any of the video, without the screen sharing, instant teleseminar and so forth, they get on the phone and have these group calls.

Anyhow, that was my first exposure, I was back in corporate America and this training environment but it definitely got the gears turning. Fast-forward a few year to 2006/2007 which obviously is about 10 years ago, that's when I started in internet marketing, I was dabbling on the side, I had done consulting by the way, up to that point doing usability and human interface design and user experience stuff; how do you make software easier to use, how do you make web pages easier to use.

I was doing consulting, so I was making very good, lucrative money as a consultant. I just started utilizing conference calls myself and then it hit me, you know I can probably use webinar technology to reach people and to not only educate them which I understood and to do client presentations but actually train and then sell, right?

This is a very familiar model to everyone now but back then it was something that was just unheard of, and I just barely started to dabble.

At that point in time I didn't invest or have much side money to go after this but I understood it, I was able to piggyback on platforms that were available to me and again that was about 10 years ago, and I actually started making money as an internet marketer by selling short reports.

My brother he comes home one weekend told me he made $3000 on the weekends selling $10 reports, it was actually at the time on the warrior forum, he sold 300 copies at 10 bucks, it was a 12 page PDF and I'm like eureka! If he can do that I can do the same thing.

So all these things Rich started to align where I've got this consulting experience on the side, I'm in corporate America at that point in time, I'm seeing this technology and thinking about teleconferences and I know that people are on stage, they're selling from the stage, I see what my brother is doing with these little PDFs and all the moon start to align, and I realized and this is where all the magic started to happen, so if someone is sort of following along at home or if someone is reading the transcript in your course or book this is the thing Rich, you get people in front of the right offer, you get the material that is of great value to them then they'll give you a lot of money.

Now, I know that sounds basic and it sounds very straightforward but let me put this in perspective of something that everyone talks about these days, funnels, let me be really clear about this.

You can sell low end products, now this is not a model for everyone, that's the caviar, right? But this is a model that definitely works. You sell low-end products; you go after a single problem with a single solution, so these are small short reports or a small training program and you sell as many units as you can, make it very compelling, if you're working with affiliates pays them handsomely, give them a 75%, give them a 100% and the idea is to bring in buyers, as many buyers in the low-end as you can, and then what you've got there is this buyer's list and they're interested in topic X, let's say it's copywriting.

Now what you can do is on your backend where the money is really made, now you run a webinar on copywriting and you make the big money, and everyone is happy about this, this is why everyone is happy.

Number one, the people that are working with you as affiliates for example, if you have affiliates, if you brought people in and they are affiliates, they're happy because they're making money handover first because they're getting 100% commissions, they're very happy about that, and maybe they're making 50% or 75% and maybe an OTO or two, an upsell or two, so they're being rewarded for the traffic, you're borrowing the traffic, they're doing just fine so they're happy.

If you have the money to spend on paid advertising, obviously that doesn't matter so much or you can use a hybrid of course, but the idea again is you get the volume of buyers in, your affiliates, you're JV partners are happy, the clients, the customers that you've brought in like with the $7 report or a $10 they're happy as well because the model is very simple, you're giving 50 or 100 or 200 dollars of value, real value to them, that's one of the open secrets, you provide something that really truly is worth 50 or 100 or 200 300 dollars for 10 bucks, and by doing that your clients and customers, these buyers that are on your list now they're happy and you've established a rapport with them where they're thrilled that they gave you money, they're happy that they turned over their hard earned money to you and that money, this is important, that money that was in their pocket is now in your pocket and it belongs there.

Rich: You're absolutely right John and I didn't mean to interrupt you but I wanted to take some time, you mentioned Citrix, in the beginning they came out with goto meeting and then added goto webinar, where goto meeting was only for 25 people, so it was more or less just basically used as a training outlet but when the webinar part came in; goto webinar, it opened up an opportunity to have 100 or 200 or 300 and now it has the capabilities of up to 1000 and there are so many other webinar platforms out there but actually you were right there at the beginning when webinar started.

Now, I want to talk about one thing because what you said is very profound and even though it's old school it can still be done today and it is basic business.

You said your brother came home and he sold 300 copies at $10 each on a product on the warrior forum and then you said I can do something like that just to get a list.

You talked about having an affiliate program where you're giving 75% or 100% which again is a great tip because now all of a sudden you've got that list and that's where the funnels or the upsells come. So now you're taking that list and you're turning it into a webinar. Did I recap that correctly?

John: That's a great summary, and Rich there's a few different things to touch on here. You've got to think, you know nowadays you hear all about hustle and grind and putting the time in and while that's true, the one missing piece is that you've got process and you've got events in your business, you've got process and you've got events and they're both equally important.

Now, one is more important in some situations and the other is more important in other situations, but the process of getting someone on to a list, getting a particular king of person, a buyer on to your list, that's a process.

You make the offer, you make the sale, they're on your list, understanding that you provide value to get someone on the list, these little tiny pieces give you what you need which is the event or the outcome or the asset, and if you take a step back you say wow, now I know how to get people on to my list, I know how to get the very best people on my list; buyers, so that's the process, right?

We can talk about funnels all day long but that's a very basic 101 funnel. Now that you've got that process or that many funnel you also have the outcome of utilizing that particular process and what's the outcome? In this case you've got some pieces like I've got the knowledge now, I've got a product and so on, but the number one asset, the number one legal piece is the buyers list.

So now what you can do now that you have the process you can expand the process, you can make it more complex, you can do all kinds of really cool stuff once you understand the process, but you can also do something Rich, and this works tremendously well with webinars.

Now you've got the asset as well which is the buyers list and now you can say to yourself geez I can build another buyers list of people who are only buying for example higher end products through your funnel or higher end products on a webinar, and the point is that you're putting together these various building blocks, you're getting lego after lego after lego. So if you just hustle and grind and just grab the money you're going to collapse, you're going to fail.

It's not just about the hustle and grind, it's not just about putting in time, it's also not just about the other end of that as well Rich, the other end of that is I'm going to plan and analyze and think and plan and get it perfect, that's just as bad, that's just as dumb, that's just as money killing as doing nothing but hustling and grinding and not realizing that you're building processes, you're getting insights and that you're able to have these building blocks.

So that's really how internet marketing works, that's how webinars work ultimately, is having an understanding.

Rich: And you're absolutely correct and nowadays everybody seems to be doing webinars. Now, we're going to talk about the process of a webinar and how to properly structure it, but I want to offer up a tip now and I want your opinion at it, it's probably something that you've already done but it seems like a lot of these new product creators or people who have these product launches, these huge product launches they miss the point by not having a webinar at the backend.

So one tip that I'm going to give everybody now, it's a tip that I use, for example you have a number one seller on JVZoo that's hit the leaderboard and sold over 1000 pieces.

If you predict or you have an idea that this is going to do well, on JVZoo specifically there's a place that you can set up for a webinar, so everyone of your buyers who have purchased that product is going to be on a webinar, now not everybody purchases the funnel.

You told everybody a little bit earlier you have to have a funnel, you start out with a $10 product and then you have a $50 product and then you upsell to another higher costing product, so what I suggest is getting in bed with somebody who has a product that you know is going to have a product launch and create a webinar for them by you hosting that webinar and giving them the opportunity to put what they already have, they know their product, they know how to put together a PowerPoint presentation, you as the host can host that webinar, not only do you get the list but you get to sell all the OTOs and benefit from that webinar, is that something you do, is that a good tip?

John: Yeah, absolutely. I'm going to break it into two different parts and here's the reason why. Ok, so if you're literally just getting started that means in the last 3 months, last 6 months or you've never made a dollar online for 2 or 3 years and now you finally do, right?

So you've got those folks that are just getting started or just experiencing success. In that case Rich, it couldn't be smarter, it really could not be smarter to partner up and to get in bed with someone who knows what they are doing with webinars, it is a brilliant move, it is extremely lucrative, you can double, triple, quadruple, quintuple the amount of money you make from your launch alone.

Forget about percentages that you would pay on the frontend, forget about percentages that you're paying or maybe even one or two upsells or anything, forget that part of your launch just for a moment and consider that if selling something for $10, heck it can be $27, many webinar products and I think most folks not everyone, many webinar products sell for like a bare minimum of 97 if not 197 these days and a lot of products that are of extremely high value; software and also coaching and training programs built in over many weeks, you're talking $500 $1000.

So take $10 product, how many sales of a $97 product make up for that? 10, right? It's a 1/10 ratio, just for a $10 to $97 product, and heck if it's a $7 product you're talking 13 14 15 times or maybe more than that.

So just consider the ratios and those folks that have come in through that frontend they're not just buyers, they are buyers interested in a specific topic and guess what advantage you have as the seller?

As Rich said if you expect to do even moderately well this is great for you because you already know what these clients and customers care about, you already know what they would have bought, keep that right in your brain, you already know what they're going to be buying.

Like I mentioned earlier as an example copywriting, you already know that you're selling a copywriting product, so you have this advantage where you're not just looking for any make money biz op type of program, you can specifically go head hunting or webinar shopping for someone who has a copywriting course or a course that will perfectly compliment the copywriting course that you are selling but at a higher level, so you already know how the moons are aligned, all you need to do is reach out to folks who are in the know and say hey- and I've got to tell you.

As a webinar product seller and Rich, I know you know this and see this all the time, as a webinar seller I am looking at, my antennas are always up for people that are moving a lot of units on the frontend, I am looking for that.

I want to work with people who are launching, because it's a hot list, so if you're launching you've got a hot list of buyers, and I want to put my training, I want to deliver value, I want to put my training in front of them and of those people I want to have them raise their hand and say yay verily I want to work with John and I'm going to fork out 200 500 thousand dollars to work with John. S. Rhodes again.

Everyone wins, the customer wins, the partner wins and you as the webinar provider or the webinar host or the webinar pitch man or the person who has the product, everyone is winning because you structured things properly, you've got the right funnel, you've got the right processes, you've got the right asset and this is the beauty Rich and I know you know this, you already know all of this, you already know how everything is going to line up because you're setting the launch up ahead of time intelligently.

And by the way JVZoo's feature of hooking into a webinar is worth not just hundreds of dollars, in many cases not even thousands, tens of thousands, so if we're looking to get to that $50,000 webinar this is a great step in that direction, not just hundreds, not just thousands but tens of thousands with the right watch. So it's a beautiful thing, you've nailed it Rich, we've nailed that.

Rich: And you know you're exactly correct. Now, here's one of the things, I cut my teeth with webinar swaps which is the JVZoo sister product which is an affiliate marketing program that you as an affiliate are able to market and sell as an affiliate to these webinars.

So let's say for example I consider myself as a webinar host, and when I say a host it's not just some guy that says ok I'm going to use my goto meeting, ok the webinar starts at 8 O'clock and it's 8 O'clock, folks here's John Rhodes, he's got a great product and go…. That's not where the secret is, the secret is if you're going to be a host what I try to tell people and train people is to treat it like you're having a radio show and you're a radio host and by doing that you're giving not only the product creator to shine but you shine as well.

One more benefit of that is most of these product creators are too busy to even think about a webinar let alone have a webinar that's attached to like $27 product that turns into a $97 OTO which turns into 199 OTO.

If you took all three of those OTOs including the main product there's your $197 product right there and for the people who have already purchased they're going to have that second opportunity to come on to a webinar where you're not only going to demo it but they'll have that opportunity to buy that OTO and the benefit for you as the host, as the person who is hosting this webinar as well as the MC, the entertainer that's presenting it you get 50% of that and these people are already buyers.

John: Yeah, that is a brilliant strategy, it's absolutely brilliant. If you already have an OTO or really a set of OTOs or upsells in place, maybe you've got most of them in place, you've got one or two other many products or reports or videos that you can add in to add a little extra juice you've already got a webinar, and it doesn't need to be a $500 price tag, it can be 77.

I mean no one says you can't sell a lower ish end product on a webinar, no one says you cannot do that, if you've already got the material, so Rich that's very brilliant, you don't necessarily have to reach out and find someone who has webinar, you don't necessarily have to put together some crazy webinar training and pitch because you've already got a bunch other training in your head, you've already got a bunch other training written if you've got a good sales letter, really great sales letters already have the right mindset, the right setup, the right kind of free training, that's a secret that a lot of people don't know.

A great sales letter which actually teach and train people and establish a rapport. My point on that is that you can take one step back, take one step back from even your frontend sales letter, take the vibe, take some of the key points in your frontend sales letter and use that for some of your training for the OTO, it's a brilliant maneuver.

Rich, I want to go back to something just for a moment, you mentioned when you're going to be a host of a webinar it's not just hand it over to someone else, hey here is Rich Wilens, hey Rich and done, you go silent. Treat it like a radio show. I want to take that sort of to the next level and this is why.

Radio shows are great when it comes to delivering content, establishing rapport, even to a degree setting yourself up as an authority and also setting up the person who is coming as an authority as well, but I want to take it just one step further and say hey, imagine that what you're doing, I want you to picture yourself doing this, imagine setting someone up for success, it's not just talking about the person, it's not just conversational or fun although those are all pieces of it and a great radio host will do these things, keep it fluid, keep it fun, but I want you to think about the positioning that you're establishing for the person who is going to train and pitch the product, the positioning and I can't stress that enough.

Because what you want to do is you want to make sure that your audience is fully aware of the firepower of the person you're bringing on, not their résumé by the way, may people fail by going through the résumé; he's been around this long, he's this smart, he's got these degrees, those things establish a certain kind of credibility and authority but they're not the selling credibility and authority and if you're not careful what you'll do is basically just list the résumé or the curriculum vitae or whatever it's called and instead rather than just kind of saying hey here's the handoff to this guy that I know you can actually elevate that person to be the rock start.

So rather than just being John Rhodes coming on it's John Rhodes, like AeroSmith, you're positioning that person up in such a way that he's the man, we'll go back again to copywriting Rich.

So Rich does an introduction, he talks about how's known me and there's this quick rapport then Rich can go into all of the money that I've made copywriting, John has made $10 million online because of his copywriting skills, John is too humble to say this but he's got over 5000 copywriting customers and the majority of them that's taken action has each made $10,000 and on and on. So what you're doing is you're talking about the benefits that I provide, so Rich is setting me up to connect with you and to position me in such a way that it's like I want those benefits, it's worth listening to this guy, because what matters more?

My college degree or the fact that my clients have regularly pulled down $10,000 for the first sales letter they ever wrote because of me, and so that's what Rich is doing, that's what Rich does as a great host, he doesn't just say hey guys look at this guy he's smart, he actually is positioning me as this incredible authority and for good reason.

Rich: You're structuring the webinar to get people to overcome their objections right from the beginning as it builds to a crescendo up to a point that's it's time to present the product and the price and that's when it's time to close.

You bring up a very good point, John, not only do you have to be a host, you have to properly educate your guest in how the format is going to run, you're going to have to get informed on what that product is and what the objections are, you're going to have to address those objections throughout the entire process not necessarily interrupting somebody on a webinar, but once you start overcoming all of these objections, when it comes time to present the sales price you know that you've overcome all of the objections and the only thing stopping you somebody hitting that buy button, so not only do you have to become a host but also you have to become a closer as well.

John: That's absolutely right. If you're worried or concerned about that as the host just keep in mind that you can always jump on the grenade, you can always do that, you can always be the person that says you can be an awe of this other person, you can just say wow I didn't know this about Rich but did you realize ..... so you can be just very humble, you can be very starry eyed and it's a very real technique, if you really didn't know how much money Rich has pulled in from a single webinar and you just found out and he's on and he's presenting, you're able to say wow!

Rich I knew that you had worked with JVZoo, so you can basically drop data, I didn't know you've done over 150 or 200 webinars, I didn't realize... and get a load of this, right?

So there is this idea, I'll end this little rampage here with this, Joe Sugarman turned me onto this idea years ago of the Greased Chute, right?

You just don't want to have any old pathway, right?

You want it to be downhill, you want it not just to be downhill, you want it to be slide, and yu want it not just to be downhill and slide, you want it to be a greased chute, so if you can take person and put them at the top, if you can set the person up at the top of the greased chute they're going to slide on down the bottom and nothing is going to stop them from ultimately hit the car or the buy button and then making that purchase, and Rich you're making a great point.

A lot of times you get the sale by removing the barriers, you remove the issues, you remove the gulches, the hang-ups, the uhms and the ahs, it's very emotional, and if you remove the objections, what's left?

If you remove every single objection and you created a greased chute, right? Because if the chute is greased and there are obstacles in the way you're still going to hit them, right?

To get to the ultimate path down to the bottom, if you remove the objections and there are no objections left at all there's nothing left.

Rich: The only thing is to hit the buy button. my favorite technique that I use and this is so not original, I started 45 years ago even though I look quite young in 1976 with Tom Hompkins, for those of you who don't know who Tom Hopkins is he's one of the icons in the sales field and especially overcoming objections and the one thing Tommy taught me and I've used this throughout my entire career, you mentioned that slide as people are going down, taking away all the objections, my two favorite words John is "other than."

Other than that is there anything stopping you from buying this product now and if they can't think of anything, well just go ahead and click that buy button because that is the right thing to do and it is what you want. Isn't it? do you not agree with that?

John: The other than is brilliant, and by the way, Rich we talked earlier about the power of having process and also having these assets, so what Rich just gave you or Rich what you just explained here very clearly is like a screw driver and there is the screw, the screw driver is other than, so if you see there's a screw all you do is go oh other than, later on there is another screw and the screws are the objections, right?

All you need to do is turn it with the screw driver, it's easy. Other than is very powerful and it's two words that encapsulates an entire process, you don't need to know neural linguistic programming, you don't need to know the nuances of hypnotic language, it's a simple language that everyone understands, in fact simple language is far superior because not only are you hitting the folks that are simple minded and there would be some and singularly focused, it works on people who have PhDs, everyone understands that, well other than that, everyone gets it, it's not difficult.

If you're person who overanalyzes, if you're a person that's looking for like the magic bullet and you try to come up with some weird crazy funnel to make something work, something is wrong, you should be looking for the other than that's available to you, so Rich that's just absolutely brilliant, I wanted to drive home that point because it's awesome.

Rich: And it's basics of selling too when you think about it. here's another thing too, 've known salesmen throughout the years that just don't get it, they sell and sell, they just don't know when to shut up or they don't know when to close, they sell for somebody else because somebody else is going to walk in after you give all that information, eliminated all the objections and then they're either going to beat you by price or personality because there are three reasons people don't buy.

People don't buy because of the personality of who's selling it, because of the product they think it sucks or the money and most of the time people love me, people love the product, money has never been the issue and if you take and utilize that process, that thought, other than that I'm here you're here the product is here, we've gone through the entire presentation, tell what's stopping us from doing business now?

And if they tell you, you go other than that, and then once you overcome it, I mean it's an awesome way to close, good technique, and by the way John I love the way you used John S. Rhodes and Aerosmith in the same sentence, it's very impressive.

So let's talk about techniques, we've talked about structure, let's talk about your process when you're either hosting a webinar or you're presenting a webinar on your own.

How do you let people know you're having a webinar, whether it's through email, Facebook ads, SEO, a registration page, any of all that. How do you start, how many emails do you send out, do you use Facebook ads?

John: I'l walk through each one of those Rich. The very first thing that I focus on in making the webinar happen is the alignment with my email list, my customers, my clients, and I learned this from James J. Jones, right?

He says, the greatest money making device in the history of mankind is this, and he holds it up, now this was years ago.

Dear friend of mine, and I'm looking at what he shows me and I'm like seriously? And he's like yeah, think about it and look at it, and what it was Rich was a calendar, he held up a calendar, it was a physical calendar, in fact you can't see it because it's off the screen here but right over there I've got my calendar and I still use it till today.

Now here is why these matters, if I've been talking about some topic, let's say it's SEO, if I've been talking about SEO it may or may not make sense to run a webinar the week and the week after.

Now I plan by the way, one two or even three or four months out of what's going to be happening and much of my marketing and much of what I do revolves around webinars, so I'm always trying to make sure that the webinar that I am going to be hosting lines up with what is on top of mind for that particular person, and I always write my emails to individuals, I'm writing to an audience of one when I write those emails, but I try to make sure that what I've been talking about over the last say, week, months lines up, so I start with the offer,

I start with the webinar, I find out who's got the best product or I revisit winners from the past, but I start there because if you don't know where you're starting, you don't know what kind of emails to write, what kind of promotions to be running on Facebook and so forth.

Now, that being said I know what the webinar is going to be about, it's on the calendar, I know who is going to be presenting it, I get all the ducks in a row about commissions and payment timing and refunds and support, I make sure all of the operational stuff is rock solid, that I know, like, trust the person, I make sure that I ask around a little bit, do my due diligence, that helps tremendously.

I get the webinar replay and I watch it, I take a look at all that stuff, ok.

Now as far as traffic goes the number way that I get traffic to my webinars and load them up is my email list, it's absolutely my email list. Now here is the magic of this, what's possible is running a webinar every single week, to some people they're like how can you possibly do that?

Well the reason is if you bring the right people on at the right time or the right offer and they run their webinar the right way you're providing tremendous value to them, in other words the training that's provided is so good, it's actually worth money, some of them will be willing to spend.

Rich: And especially for your list, the most important thing is building a rapport with your list. People don't really care how much you know until they know how much you care.

If you have a list that you're just sending offer after offer without giving them any kind of value content or something free, you'll wind up losing these people and so what you said is very valid, if you give a different webinar on what the interest are in your list every week you're providing to your list information that they won't be able to get anywhere else, and who better to buy from.

You know, people are going to trust a person that they know and if they are on your list you need to build that rapport, so when you do say hey I'm recommending this, this is a John S. Rhodes recommendation they'll go ahead without question and they'll hit that buy button.

John: That's right, so you've actually killed two or three birds with one stone. You do want to provide free value, I think it's Evan Payne who said hey let's push the free line and idea of being able to mail literally every single day if you want as long as you're providing value, you don't always have to get paid, right?

And you can do that with webinars, and it's something that many people ignore, they forget about is that, you know, you're sending an email out, you're trying to get people registered, as long it's not a pitch fest and just sell sell and sell and totally blind, if the people you're bringing on the training is rock solid, even though it's a train and pitch webinar what's the first part of that?

The training, it solves the paradox, it really does, it solves the paradox of mailing every single day on something that people are going to buy, like every single email that you send out in my opinion ought to be selling something but keep in mind, and I said this earlier about sales page is rich, a sales page should be so good that by the time you're done reading the sales page you've learned something; a trick, a technique, an approach, a mindset, well the exact same thing happens but at a higher level, a more robust and more enriching level with a webinar, that's a paradigm shift that made a difference in the amount of money that I was making early on, going from just selling reports and really low end training to webinars.

I'm like wow I can provide tremendous value myself on my webinars to the people I bring on, and there is diversity in the people I bring on, so my list ends up loving me, they really end up loving me despite every single email that goes out being related to ultimately making money and getting the sale.

That's because I providing value along the way or bringing people that provide value. So the emails that go out, in that email itself, in the body of the email I'm educating, training, I'm also entertaining, it's edutainment, I'm educating and I'm entertaining, I'm giving a glimpse into my life, how I've made money, what's going on in my family, I'm providing some value and I'm also getting people over to the registration page.

The registration page generally don't offer a lot of values in of themselves in trying to get people on to the webinar but it's pretty profound that you can have an email that has value in it, and you're sharing part of your life, you get people over to the webinar registration page and then getting them sign up for the webinar.

So I use email for that, my number one method is my email list Rich but I do use a couple of other techniques as well, go on unless you wanted to make a point.

Rich: I do want to make a point and because that's very profound, back in the days of webinar swaps and by the way you mentioned James Jones. James Jones has made hundreds of thousands of dollars, my partner, my mentor and my good friend E. Brian Rose before JVZoo or webinar swaps even existed he had a product called Google red carpet, do you remember that John?

John: Absolutely.

Rich: And went on to James Jones and the first time on a live webinar he made $60,000 and I think over $100,000 on the replays. So with that being said when had the opportunity to take over webinar swaps I blotted my own personality, I had to do the main, I had to set it up, it was a job but within that job I had to do something different because people were now discovering webinars and they were going ok, I want to jump on this band wagon, what can I do differently that will enhance not only webinar swaps but eventually JVZoo as well, and you talk about letting in a piece of personal information. I used to open up my webinar 15 minutes early, so for example if the webinar is going to be at 8 O'clock eastern time which by the way if you're going to say it's going to be 8 O'clock eastern time you damn well better make sure you start it at 8 O'clock eastern time.

What's more insulting when someone says you know what? It's 8 o'clock, most of the people are still there, and they go what, this is insulting to me, I showed up at 8 o'clock, I don't have to wait for 10 minutes, but I used to open it up 15 minutes early and the reason for that is I'll do a kind of pre-show, kind of get to know you.

This way it doesn't take away from the 8 o'clock starting time, how you are doing, where you're from, I've done this, I've done that and you build a rapport as well, so you're exactly right when you have to leave a little bit of personal information with your list because people buy people and if they like you they'll buy from you, and you know what? You're on a predesdent, John, and anybody who does webinars and anybody who has a list, you should respect that list; you should build a list and build a rapport.

John: Yeah, I want to piggy back on something and then I'll continue on the other ways that I fill up webinars.

So you had mentioned at starting 8 O'clock and insulting people, it's absolutely true and I want you to think about something, imagine you're going on a first date, let's say someone just gets on your email list for the very first time, very similar to that first date, maybe a little bit different but similar enough.

If you're going to tell the girl or the guy that you're going to be there 8 o'clock you better show up, if you show up late unless you've got a great excuse which you probably don't, you better be there not only on time but a little bit early, you better get your ducks in a row, you better make sure you do that, and this is the reason why, it took me a while to figure out the exact reason why.

The analogies are nice and the dating stuff is fine and you're insulting people, but you think about the why, the why those matter.

What you've told someone, because they know this is an event, they know there are other people on the webinar, so if you don't start at 8 O'clock that you said you were going to, what you're telling the people that were there before 8 is that you're not as important as the people that are showing up late.

Think about that, you're actually insulting them because you're saying even though you showed up early you're not as important as someone who shows up late, so it's a double whammy.

Not only have you insulted them by saying you're a lesson pawn but you're also training your list to show up late, like hey, next time I should show up late because he or she caters to people who show up late, so it's a double whammy, it's not only insulting because you're saying being early is stupid and being late is cool and you shoot yourself in the foot too and something else.

Some people do have hard deadlines for getting on and off of webinars, not just your audience but also your presenter. If you're running a type ship what does that say about how well you pay people, what does that say about how good your support is, what does that say about your character in general?

So that's the reason why and that's important, it's not oh you're insulting, you're training people up to show up late and you're devaluing the people that are more valuable because they can show up on time and they are reliable, so that is truly important Rich. So the traffic, as well as the campaign goes I usually email approximately two days before, sometimes three days before, sometimes one day before, depends on my mailing schedule for other promotions I've got going on and obligations and family life and so forth, but typically it's about two days before, and I try to mail them in the morning two day before.

If I'm really pushing hard I might do a re-mail two days out, that night for folks who can open, one day same thing, try to mail in the morning and if it makes sense I might mail out at night and then in the day of I'll mail or two times depending on the time of day. So two days out and of course there's the replay.

Rich: How many times in the day, do you mail in the morning, do you mail an hour out, 10 minutes or live? How many times?

John: Typically I'll end up mailing twice, I'll mail as early as I think it is rational and reasonable, so to me pretty early the day of, in the morning and it doesn't matter if it's 2 O'clock or 3 O'clock in the afternoon or 7 or 8 at night.

Anywhere from an hour or half an hour before I'll say hey we're starting soon, and in some situations I would say hey jump on now, I'll literally say jump on now 5 or 10 minutes before, it kind of depends on how hard I've been mailing and how aggressive I've been.

If I haven't been very aggressive I'll be very aggressive right before and then vice versa, I try not to be aggressive aggressive aggressive, meaning like lots of emails and timing and jump on and scarcity and do it now, I tend to try to increase the pressure as we go because you want people to jump on right when they should jump on.

It's better to start off light and then increase the pressure, not always possible to do that but that's what I tend to like to do. The other thing that I like to do Rich and this is really important is I like to exploit technology and platforms to my advantage, and what I mean specifically here at least with goto webinar and I know other platforms can do some of this as well is I would go in to goto webinar and make very small changes to goto webinar; the title and then I will utilize that to send out another mailing from the system, from goto webinar not from me, that's like a $10,000 tip right there.

Rich: And let me specific about that too. If you're going to start your webinar in a few minutes what you do in goto webinar specifically, you got to the edit page of your webinar before you start your webinar and then you can change the titles of your webinars. So you change the title of your webinar, you can say starting now or starting in 5 minutes or starting in 2 minutes, then when it has a spot or little button that says click to notify registrants, you click that and it automatically sends it out to all your registrants. So people who are already signed up for the webinar are going to see it again and more important you're not considered spamming them or just throwing out emails, it's coming from the system itself. That's a great tip John.

John: Yeah, and it's friendly. I do want to put a caveat out there, you know. You're not trying to fool anyone, people like to have these reminders, we're all busy and so an email that's coming from in this case the system; out of goto webinar is not very aggressive.

I mean you can be pretty aggressive in your title but it's not seen as the same kind of aggression as your email, it's more of a friendly reminder, you know why? It's like outlook, I don't use outlook anymore but if you were using outlook it's like ping!

There's an alert or if you're using gmail or Google calendars or whatever you're just getting an alert effect like hey this is just a reminder whereas when you send an email you're like hey get on, do this and you're selling or being perceived as selling but when it comes to the system that's not the case.

That's the first part, the second part of that is when the emails comes from in this case goto webinar; from the system you're already mailing to someone who has signed up and raised their hand officially, so it really truly is a reminder, it's not hey you need to register and then show up, it's more like just show up, so the level of aggression is significantly lower and a lot friendlier and people are already trained to do that.

Ok, shifting gears to what else I do, I use Facebook and I use Facebook in three or four different ways, so let me walk through each one kind of quick, we can dive into each one if it makes sense.

So one of the first things I did is I had to reboot my business, I rebooted my business for a variety of reasons, nothing bad just business circumstances changed and so forth. I rebooted my business fully and completely backed out on my own starting from scratch and it includes my email list and everything else, and one of the things that I did immediately was I set up a Facebook fan page.

Facebook fan page is very specifically meant for promotions, I talk an awful lot about webinars, my frontend products as well but I talk about webinars, I give people links to webinars but I have that Facebook fan page and I continuously try to grow that and it's also a place for me to have social conversations and social connections with folks as it related to webinars and my products.

So, it's an addition to my emails that are going out, it's another platform or another mechanism for reaching to people but very importantly socially interacting with them.

Ok, that's part of it, the other reason why I do that is that when you have a fan page and it's all about marketing and selling and it's all about what you do, your product, your service, if it's sort of focused that way and you get people liking and you get people sharing, what happens is you don't only get free traffic because people are talking and they are sharing your material but it lowers your ad cost, it lowers your advertising cost with Facebook because the more folks that you've got liking your page, like your posts literally the lower the amount that you have to pay reach people.

Facebook rewards people that spend time and money and energy of course on Facebook, so Facebook likes Facebook, Facebook enjoys money being spent on Facebook, so I spend a reasonable amount of time building up my Facebook fan page.

Rich: We'll emphasize that in a minute. Do you use a Facebook page, I know you have the fan page but let's say you're doing a specific webinar, do you set up a specific fan page for that particular webinar or do you just concentrate on your own fan page?

John: Yeah, I concentrate on my own and I will tell this though, in the past what I've done and it's a great technique, just right now doesn't fit my business rhythm, my business model and the flow of what I am doing now.

What you can do Rich and this is totally cool, is you can set up either a fan page or a group and I've done both and you bring people in for that specific webinar, and if it's a group like a secret group you only allow people into that, they end up either going to that webinar and then you can sell them, you can use that for presales or you can use it as a bonus and say hey, if you want to get into this group you have to go to the webinar, you have to invest but once you're in this is where you get my private coaching.

So there's lots of different models that you can use for providing value to people, for attracting people, for keeping certain people out, so get creative as it makes sense for your business.

Rich: It's also a reason to buy John because I know people who just specifically buy products just to get in the Facebook group alone, so it's an excellent tool not only for providing value but providing follow up and of course upsells down the road for the rest of your products.

John: Right. Let me give like a little insider tip, I've done this a few times and it has worked out really well and it's probably the first thing that I would do if I was getting into groups again. It's the bonus that you can provide, it's great if you can provide a bonus on a webinar if you're like hey what can I provide on a webinar as a bonus?

So you're the host and someone else is training and pitching, one of the very best bonuses and this is very much in line with what Rich just said is you say I am going to give you access to this private group but not just private access to the group.

There's actually two ways to do this, you can answer their specific questions from your point of view and everything that you know, basically just kind of doing some coaching, that's usually what people think of but there is a secret within a secret there which is hey guess what?

I'm going to be using the technique and the software and the tools that being presented and being sold to you, I'm just like you are and we're going to go through this together, and I know that you get the software and the training and the coaching and the bonuses from the dude-

Rich: The presenter

John: I'm going to go through that with you, look over my shoulder as I go through this, so you're going to get a live real world case study as I go through this. Now this comes with some risk, you have to be careful about how you do that, how you position-

Rich: And you actually have to do it as well.

John: You have to deliver. If a person is on a webinar with you and that person likes you a lot, Rich said it, people buy people, and here's the thing, if they're buying that product because of you, you can really set yourself up for a massive success by doing that, and by the way I have done this where the particular method or system that I am going through, guess what?

It really makes money and becomes a true passive income or side income or something that I can sell off to someone else or use as a future bonus because you're building an asset.

So it's really valuable to set up these groups and fan pages for those purposes. Now, I will tell you without a doubt that the very best Facebook traffic that I have experienced is from custom audiences from my email list. So you take your email list, you drop it, I don't have time to go through it obviously, but you take your email list and you drop it in your Facebook and Facebook marries up those email addresses with the profiles within Facebook and then you can specifically target those people in your Facebook ads, very specifically.

These are the same people that are on your email list, now you might be saying well John they're already on my email list so why would I double or triple market that?

Well you've heard how many times if you've been around the block at all, even one time, you've heard that people have to hear the message over and over, they have to hear it seven times, they have to hear it twenty times, they have to see it again and again, well it's just true.

Some people are not going to get your emails, you emails will go to spam, they're not being delivered, their email address change, it goes on and on, right?

So even though you love your email list and you like to send the people one to one some people are just not going to see it but they're going to see it on Facebook and the cost is very low.

Now the second best audience that I found is a very targeted audience related to you and related to the topic and again without going into all the nuances and split testing and everything else, you can really target those folks who have liked your fan page, right?

Again we're talking about the email list, the custom audience being number one, number two are those folks who have interacted with you and have liked your fan page. Again you might say John all I need to do is update my fan page, right? And my answer is kind of sort of but not everyone, I mean Facebook does not show your fan page to the world, it's like 2% of everyone, right?

But here's the thing, if you pay money you can target that specific Facebook fan page that you've set up and that's again much cheaper clicks that just kind of spray out to Facebook as a whole, that's the second most lucrative.

Third most lucrative is you go after folks who are interested in a particular topic, copywriting and then you kind of zero in on the better countries out there, tier one countries and so forth but that's much more difficult to do.

However by doing that, there's some magic in doing that, by doing that you can bring I brand new people to your list, you can bring in brand new people that you wouldn't have reached otherwise, so it's kind of like a pyramid, right? Under one hand super focused, super cheap with email, less focused less cheap with your fan page and even less focused and less cheap ultimately for going that broad but in terms of net new people that you're connecting with, the triangle the funnel is almost inverted, right?

Because if they're already on your list they're already on your list so you're not getting anyone new, if they're already a fan then it's kind of modeling in the middle but if you bring someone in totally outside they're net new to your list if you do it right.

So pros and cons, and by the way if you ask what I like the best, I like going after my list folks the most because it's most lucrative to me but I really do use the other two tiers because I want to bring in new people, I want to make new associations and it just plane works.

Rich: And it builds the list as well, that's the most important thing. What's a good time for you, what time do you hold your webinars, do you like holding in the afternoon by 3 O'clock, 8 O'clock eastern, 7 O'clock, you tell me?

John: I've got two different time slots that I like the best, I'm in the central time zone so what I like to do is 2pm eastern, 1pm central if I'm doing one in the afternoon, and there's different reasons for this, some of it is testing, some of it is just habits, some of it is like bio rhythms, right?

What works for me, some of it is just thinking through my primary audience, basically US based but I do have folks in other parts of the world, you know, Europe obviously, and if I'm doing let's say 2pm eastern you're looking at 7pm or 8pm in Europe which is pretty damn good, right?

And in the US roughly speaking I'm working around lunch time right to 1, noon, depending on time zone, so I'm working between lunch time and break time, also break time a little bit on the eastern. So it's a pretty good time, like 10am eastern terrible, right? 4pm or 5pm eastern people are starting to drive home, they commute.

By the way on the west coast if you're trying to do anything really before 4 and 6 Pacific Time, trust me people have commutes and you've got to keep that in mind, if you don't care about the west coast then it will hit rush hour.

Rich: But you know John in defense of that people are now starting to listen to these webinars on their mobile devices whether it's an ipad or coming through the speakers in their car, so you can also look at hey this is for all of you in LA that's stuck on the freeway. that's going to take you an hour and half to get home it's also a benefit as well. Not something that's your priority but something that people might listen to when they are in the car stuck in traffic.

John: Yeah, and one of the things that relates very much to that Rich is you need to anticipate and expect that although you're having a live event that many people are looking for a replay, that want the replay.

I'm not going to talk about replays per say and all that right now but what I do want to point out that's super important is that people that are listening and can't buy that live event you're selling on and you're trying to be intelligent about your positioning and so forth, you're actually not selling you're preselling, you're actually preselling.

To your point Rich about people listening through ipad, iphone or their mobile device or however it is that they're listening in, they might have a very strong intention to buy but they can't.

Also they want to have their wife, husband, partner, grandparents, kids, whatever, they want to have someone else listen and they might be the ones that are doing the vetting, is it worth it for my partner to hear this for example, so-

Rich: Let me just jump on one quick second because you mentioned something that was a good point. I hear sometimes as an objection

well I've listened to your whole webinar but I want to check with my wife, so my question would be to them and this is perfect in overcoming objections.

Well if your wife said yes what would you do? Well I would buy it, well you know what?

You've got a 30 day money back guarantee, go ahead and buy it and show it to her later, she would love you and appreciate it and if she doesn't like it go ahead and take advantage of the guarantee; perfect way to overcome that objection.

John: Yeah, and you can do some fun stuff with that, you can actually play around and say hey look, who wears the pants in the house?

And you know it increases your sexual power your sexual strength by showing your decisiveness. So the 2pm eastern, 1pm central for me, I like that time slot. The other time slot that I like a lot is either 7pm or 8pm eastern, right?

I know that does run into the rush hour on the west coast, that's ok, I know that and I know how to word things and we talked about that a moment ago.

 I actually try to do as much as I can in the middle of the day, I try my very hardest to do that 2 O'clock, it's my favorite time spot. I'm on at that point, it really works well for me, it works well for my host, I don't have to worry about it getting to be 9 10 11 O'clock at night, I don't mind staying up late but I try to be aware of other folks who are listening in or maybe it's dinner time or maybe my host has social activities and so forth.

So it's become my second choice, my first choice used to be that time spot but now it's really my second choice, my primary choice is by 2 O'clock mostly for personal reasons and the results seem to be as good as if not better than at night and then the second choice is 7pm or 8pm eastern.

Mornings are terrible, mornings do not work, for me they really never have, late afternoons are garbage, around lunch time and just after dinner, and if you know your audience, if you know most of your folks are in whatever time zone you can do the analysis on that then structure your time around your customers and clients and your email list.

Rich: What's your opinion on replays? Some people say you have a replay and you can double your money, other people say well I don't send out replays, what do you say?

John: Let's kind of break it into two scenarios, right? So the first scenario is that your webinar truly is part of a larger campaign and if your webinar is part of a larger campaign, what I mean by that is let's say you're sending out emails, you're getting folks on, you're going to send out maybe a PDF, follow along or maybe a transcript and maybe you've got some extra bonuses that you've already planned on that you're going to reveal, almost like a Jeff Walker product launch formula where you release something brand new, you can turn a webinar not just from a singular event but into a 5 6 7 day event.

 it's a whole process and if you're doing that then you've got to make that decision, then it comes down to that first decision. I'm I going to put a webinar out there that has nothing but it's raw, there's scarcity, I want people to buy on this webinar then you say hey there's no replay, maybe the last day in the sequence, it's the very last day to buy, in that case no replay or maybe it might be in the middle, you might say look, I can't do a replay because, you always need a because not just to be a jerk but you need a because like well, I'm going to show numbers on the screen so that it can get kind of tricky and fancy here and say, I'm going to show numbers on the screen that are private and I can't have them out in the public domain, I can't leave them out there, so it truly is live and I'll never show these numbers again, these technique again.

So it can get clever and fancy and it can be all the fun to do that. In other cases, again in terms of this campaign idea you might do nothing but live event after live event and you can do that in a couple of different ways, so the live event is live event and never again.

Next live event on a different set of topics but similar, again and again, so if you love live events and you want to do it that way you can.

Now, here's another things that you can do, I'm just putting options out there for a minute and then there is one other piece here. Video option that's really an awful lot of fun is you run the webinar and it's a great live webinar and then you have a rebroadcast or a live encore, so it's the exact same webinar, it's not an evergreen webinar by the way, you take the exact same webinar and you run it again, you play the video of the webinar you did a day or two previous, it is live because you are on the webinar, maybe the presenter is on as well, but you're on the webinar and you're answering questions, right?

You're not doing it verbally, you're not speaking but you're in the chat box in the Q&A, you're very heavily interacting. These semi live rebroadcasts are extraordinarily powerful, very lucrative, they're better in some cases than the actual live event, they're better than replays in many cases because of the interaction and yet the work that you have to do is cut into like a third, maybe a quarter.

Rich: You've brought up a very important point and I believe that you need to work the question box, people have questions and even though, and I have two opinions on this. Number one, you should know what questions and what objections prior to your presentation because you can give them to the host and he can ask those questions at a particular time so that you can actually overcome those objections when you're building the structure.

The other thing is when you're doing that live encore you are live because you're answering the questions in real time and people know that, people know when it's a phony webinar, when it's a replay because they're asking questions and there is no body there to answer, so I totally agree with that.

John: Yeah, and you know what is really powerful about this? You can pull back the curtain; open the kimono, you can do these things at the beginning of the live rebroadcast, you can be very blunt and say, just so you know, the webinar you're about to see and experience was recorded yesterday, we're going to replay it for you but make no mistake, I and my team and Rich we're literally all here and guess what?

Rather than presenting and having to worry about the technology guess what we're going to do? We're going to focus 100% on you and your questions for your business, so we're here live.

So you can actually use some judo and use some momentum and actually lay it all out on the table and say it actually is a replay but we are here, the humans behind this, we're here to help you out with that, so you can use a little bit of some psychological judo to make things work.

So back to the replays just for a moment, I really like to give people replays and it's pretty variable, right? So what I have found, and you can get all fancy pants and tricky on the webinar and then editing the video afterwards for the replay, you can use on webinar scarcity techniques and there's bunch of stuff that you can do, like hey if you're on this webinar right now on Saturday the 21st… or you can say things that are a little bit more in-between, you can say things like hey if you're hearing my voice right now, if you're experiencing this webinar in this way like I am I want to give you these bonuses.

So again we can get into the nuances of the language that you use on the webinar to increase or decrease scarcity and get people to order and handle objections, but in any of that.

For the replay itself I have found that it's anywhere from about a 50% bump upwards of about a 200% bump, meaning that if I made a 5000 on a webinar I'm going to add another 2500 to another 10 grand, right? It does swing but basically never zero, you're always going to make money on the replay, at least one, you're going to make something on the replay.

In other cases just depending because it's one of these topics, maybe the topic that the presenter is presenting, right? Some people need to think these things over.

The presenter can sort of grow on people, the topic can grow on people, some times the barrier is maybe you're working around the holiday, in other cases maybe what you're doing is selling something that is really high price and they need to see again and again, they need to get the PDF, they need to get the extra bonuses, you need to stack the value over a period of time after the first webinar, but it's typically, I know it sounds like a wide range but it's a much less wide range, but you can bump the amount you make by profit 50% - 200%, it's gone over that for me in the past but 50 – 200, that's a very typical range that you'll see.

Rich: How long do you keep the price up? Do you keep it up till let's say it's on a Thursday, do you keep it Sunday at midnight; 24hours, 48hours, give me an idea of what John S. Rhodes does.

John: If it is on a Thursday it will run exactly through a Sunday night, I like ending on Sundays, people are kind of zeroed in on that day, they've had time to get through the weekend and the hubbub and they're also thinking about going back to work on Monday and how they get their freedom, so you think about the psychology of what happens on Sunday, right?

If they went to their place of worship on Sunday, there's also some things going on there, abundance mindset and just clarity in the world and go to a different level in a different way, so they're sort of the psychological tools that you have are different on a Sunday I think.

Another thing too is that they had the fun of a weekend and that's carrying over to Sunday as well, the energy in other words from a Thursday to Friday into Saturday, there's a lot of very positive energy that's happening that you're still carrying over that you're capitalizing on as a webinar host and also they're thinking about Monday at the same time, it's just a great time.

That being said, I don't like ending on Mondays, I don't like ending on Saturdays, people are not just as tuned in, I tend to like activity when I am producing or I'm shutting down on Tuesdays and Thursdays, Wednesdays ehh, Friday s ehh.

I was very successful for years with Jay Boyer running webinars on Fridays because no none was doing them, so you can find slots that makes sense as well but if I had to say to someone who is just starting out I would say look at Tuesday as far as running webinars or ending webinars, look at Thursdays as far as starting and ending webinars and look at Sundays for ending webinars or doing certain value bumps and look at maybe Friday and Saturday for live replays or Tuesdays or Thursdays for live replays as well but be aware of what's going on in the regular work week and how you drop your webinars and the replays should line up with the rhythm of a typical work week; Monday to Friday, will happen Saturday, will happen Sunday and think of how that falls in, so those are great days; Tuesday s, Thursdays, Sundays and the manner the days went through.

Rich: Now you just mentioned those, that's the end of the webinar; let's work back a little bit. What are the better days for you to actually have a webinar; Tuesday, Thursdays, Wednesdays, Mondays?

John: Yeah, I probably like Thursdays the best, Wednesdays aren't too bad, Tuesdays I like but I do Tuesdays if I'm going to run a very short webinar.

So let me run through two typical scenarios. The most typical scenario is for me to try and do something on Thursday, typically for me it's like 2 O'clock if I can do it if not I would do it as I had mentioned; 7pm or 8pm and then I close the webinar out after the replay or and the live encores on Sunday night at midnight. My second choice is going to be on a Tuesday in the afternoon, it's going to be a short webinar meaning a short cycle and I'm going to end on Thursday, and by the way for the mailings for that my normal typical mailings for a Thursday is going to be Tuesday Wednesday to get folks on, right?

I already mentioned that, and then on Thursday and then replay and close on Sunday. If I'm running a short webinar I'm going to start mailing on Monday, I'll be pretty aggressive. I'll mail Monday, I'm going to mail Tuesday for the webinar of course, replay or live rebroadcast on Wednesday and then close out hard on Thursday.

I like closing out hard on Thursdays if I've done a Tuesday webinar just because- part of it is my list and how I've trained my list up, that's a very important factor Rich, is how is your list trained up with how you operate and your time zones and everything else.

I must have given you my examples, one is that longer sequence and then the other is that shorter sequence but I'll move them around if I have to, I'll move it based on the folks that I'm hosting, I'll move it around based on personal stuff, I'll move it around based on holidays, but those two cycles are pretty typical for me to run.

Rich: How important is follow-up to you, do you follow up? Let's the webinar is over but you still have this list, I mean does it go on to just a basic list for you or do you actually specifically try to follow up with these people as to well I know you didn't buy or whatever reason it is, you mail them. How do you do your follow up?

John: My follow-up is very basic and pretty much always has been and I do know that other people have gotten relatively sophisticated with their follow ups.

I tend to keep things pretty simple so that the operation of my business is more simple, I would rather make less money and have a simpler life and a repeatable process, that's me. And also the expenses and the time don't make sense for where I'm at.

Now as the business continues to grow I'll start considering these follow-ups. By the way there is something that I've done with people that are more sophisticated, and there are folks that are more sophisticated with their funnels, there's a whole variety of reasons for that, and if that's the case many times I would say hey, I've done this with James Jones, I've done this with a lot of people but with folks that I trust, folks that I know who are good with webinars if not great, if not super great; all-stars.

If I know they know what they're doing and that they are going to treat the list the right way I would want them to capture my leads, I will mail in to the webinar that I'm hosting, so it's my email, my folks who are registering but I would let the other person capture the leads and allow them to follow up with those leads right along with me.

In some cases I would say hey you take care of all the follow-up, in some cases I would say we're both going to follow up, in other situations I would say hey when we're done with this promotion burn the list, delete the list, in other cases I would say no, fair and square, keep the list.

So it depends, this is the importance of being a cool cat, this is the importance of establishing a rapport with people you're doing business with.

If they are cool you let them capture the leads, if you know they're going to sell more, treat your leads right and not just spam them to death with all kinds of offers that don't make any sense, but if you're cool, you let them do that and by the way it's not always tit for tat or back scratching or quid quo pro but there is a likelihood that if you do that for them that when you have a product and they host you it will come back the other way.

It's not a requirement, I don't ask for it, but if it's possible and it makes sense you can also build your list that way. People say John how can I build my list?

I'm like run webinars; this doesn't make any sense, how? Capture the leads, just be cool about that and find ways of capturing the leads and then doing that. Back to the core question though, Rich just to be really clear, my follow-up is very basic, I keep the follow up very targeted and focused on the replay and those folks that are net new coming on to the list they get added to the general list because guess what, next week is going to be another mini promotion and I'm going to add on very likely a webinar as well, so they know, they get to know like a radio show, they know I'm going to have a webinar very likely on a Tuesday or Wednesday.

It's going to be a great training, great value and so on. So they get to know pretty quickly I'm doing webinars and providing training and bonuses and follow-ups and replays and analysis and doing stuff on the fan page and so forth.

Rich: How important are bonuses, you mentioned bonuses there. I've seen a lot of people throwing bonuses, sometimes they're really weird bonuses, they're PLR bonuses, they're really bonuses that really aren't worth much and yet there are some bonuses that are. What's your opinion on bonuses in order to get the person to buy now?

John: You've really hit on all the critical pieces; let's kind of think this through. If you provide a bonus that subtracts value then you've done some serious damage to yourself and serious damage to your list.

What I mean by that is Rich you had mentioned low quality not high quality but low quality PLR (private label rights), it's a product that they might know about it they might not but if they found out it was a $7 product and you didn't add any value to it, you just kind of grabbed it off the shelf and gave it to them, that doesn't make an awful lot of sense.

Number two of that is if it's not in alignment with the product and the intention of the product, it's just a grab bag; it's a double whammy, right?

So not only is it low quality but it doesn't even line up to the webinar and the offer, ok. So here's another thing, next on the bonus train because there's a lot of pieces to this.

The next thing is that you want the bonus to not compete with the offer itself, and this is what I'm talking about, and I used to make this mistake and I felt really dumb about it, and I remember specifically I had hosted someone and it was all about Facebook traffic. I hosted them thy did a great job, it was a great offer, it was actually PLR, it was decent PLR and I jacked it up, I added some videos to it but it was good, I thought it was good but this is what ended up happening.

I ended up competing with the product because my PLR product and even though with my videos even though it was my way and so on, it ended up being this additional content and material that detracted from this other person.

I started being positioned in such a way that I was knocking this person down, I was knocking down the presenter, I was knocking down their product and they were like John! And this is how I learn.

I saw in the comment box people asking if they could just buy my bonus, they realized they didn't need the product; I was like oh no. so I sabotaged my sales by putting a competing bonus out there. So don't try to fat pile on, just keep stacking on a bonus.

If you've got a traffic webinar don't try to put on the same kind of traffic offer, what I should have done in this case going after another Facebook traffic training, I should have said you know I love

Facebook combined with YouTube, here's what I'm going to add, it's my secret source, YouTube traffic technique and oh by the way not just as another traffic technique it works best and in fact it only works when you combine it with Facebook, you got it, did you see what I did there?

So not only is it separate but it works best in combination with, it's like lock and key, you've unlocked this extra bonus, this extra value, it is still traffic but it's different, works best with, complements and supplements, doesn't replace, doesn't try to fat pile or stack on to that. So that's the secret within the secret Rich is that if you're going to do a bonus make sure the bonus is truly a valuable bonus, it's in alignment with the offer but it doesn't beat the crap out of the offer itself otherwise you would lose sales

Rich: Do you ever utilize sms or phone to remind people that they're having a webinar?

John: I used to in the past, now this is years and years ago and ran into some problems and actually some colleagues of mine ran into this problem as well, unless you're really on top of the technology what will end up happening is you'll end up sending out messages to people at the wrong time, I don't mean like fat finger it, I mean literally it's 3am and they get a text message or a phone call and they're like hey what happened, so you can do it, it's extremely lucrative to do It but you really have to be on top of it, you yourself need to be on top of it or it needs to be in hands of someone that you really trust.

Now, what I will say is even though I don't currently utilize that technology if I was going to get into it again and I might in the next 6-12 months, if and probably when I do that, the most likely use of phone and text technology should actually be leading up to the webinar not just for the reminder though, for the sale. What I'm saying is you can send a note and hey I would like to buy that product, text your offer in.

Frank Kern is doing a great job at doing exactly that, hey send a note to the girls in the office, they're better looking than I am and they'll give you a better deal, right? So if I'm going to be using sms, texting and phone centers and so forth it will be for the sake of closing the sale not to get people on to webinars or trying to make that work, I want it to be part of the sale process but not the mechanism to get people on or to show up at right time, it just never worked out the way that I wanted it to work out and ticked off people on the list in different time zones that had no reason to get the messages that they got.

Rich: John it's been a wonderful hour and half, I am so happy that you came on but I don't want to let you go without getting a little bit more words of wisdom.

Most of the people who are listening or reading the transcript or reading the book they're going ok, those are a lot of great tips but I don't think John has told us everything. What in particular or what can you add that will be a great tip whether it's to increase people staying on the webinar till the end, whether it's to increase people showing up to the webinar, whether it's when do you do you do the closing or how long the webinar should be or if follow-up is necessary, how often do you follow up with this particular product? I know that's a lot, let's tackle it.

John: I'll go after one secret one tip and I'm glad it's at the end. No one wants to hear this, no one likes this, if anyone says they like it they're like in the top 2%, they're literally are. People tend to hate this, they're not good at it, they're very resistant to this, but this is truly for me as a webinar host the number one money maker, it's truly the number one money maker but I usually don't tell people, and Rich the reason I don't tell people is because they hate it so much, and it comes down to this, it's operations.

I'm not talking about the webinar setup, I'm not talking about the replay page, I'm not talking about the support link or URLs or signing up for the affiliate program or vetting people. I don't mean that, I'm not talking about the operations for the overall webinar being structured, I'm talking about the operation webinar itself. Now you hinted on this earlier, you said you've got to really watch the Q&A, you have to watch the chat, and I've got to tell you the number one tip for maximizing the money as a webinar host is being in tune with the people that are on the webinar live.

You'll make more money by really tuning in to what people are doing on that webinar, and here's the beauty of the operational excellence, here's the beauty of it, they're telling you what their objections are, they're letting you know what their frustrations are, they're sharing of themselves and their personality and you're able to literally in no other way in real time one to one connect with them.

o this is the secret within the secret, right? So that's the secret, but what does it mean to be operationally excellent? Use their first name, I know that's basic; I know what's basic Rich but use their first name. Every single time I respond to someone if they ask question I say hey Rich,… or here's the URL Tom… drop it in, I'll be very personal, I say hey that's a great question, I thank them, hey congratulations you've done a great thing, I'm non-stop interacting with them as the webinar host.

The other thing I'm able to do, remember if we go back to the beginning we talked about being that radio show host or being the announcer and setting up Aerosmith for coming up on stage or John S. Rhodes coming up on the virtual stage, right?

And what you're doing is you're positioning and setting the person up, so operational excellence also includes this. If I'm hosting and Rich was presenting, in the chat box throughout the entire presentation I'm like wait till you see what Rich has in store for you.

Rich has solved that problem, hang on for just a couple of minutes because I know he's going to answer that exact question, all you have to do is just hold on for another few minutes because Rich is going to answer that, oh great question, everyone needs to hear this, during the Q&A.

I'm going to bring up your question Sally, Sally I really appreciate that, I'm actually going give Rich that question live, so you can hear the name, but there's a little bit more here Rich.

There is a secret within the secret within the secret, I want to flip it around and if was presenting, so Rich is hosting, John S. Rhodes is presenting, what I do as a presenter and this is like being an octopus mentally but it truly is the most lucrative things you can possibly do out of everything.

Now I said operational excellence, I said interacting one to one and so forth, the smartest thing you can do and actually I was so happy, it was Anthony Morrison, Anthony Morrison said this out loud to me and I just high fived the guy, I just high fived him because you know how many people I've told that to?

I said very few because they don't get it or they can't do it, so the best of the best do this and if you can master this Rich, this can double your conversions if not triple your conversions, I'm not bullshitting, I'm absolutely not bullshitting.

This is what you do, as the webinar presenter, as long as you can multitask not crazy but as long as you can multitask and watch the Q&A box, keep your eyes on your presentation if you're doing like a Google hangout or one to one that's fine too, but if you're able to watch the Q&A box and look over, I have two monitors; I've got my main monitor and my other one, and I'm watching, looking over and I see objections coming in Rich.

I see the objections coming in, do you know what I do? What I do is I look at the objection, the wheels are turning and as part of my presentation and as close to real time as I possibly can, when I see that objection I smoothly answer the objection by providing the answer in the training and I never actually bring up the objection, I just answer the objection.

So let's say that Sally just said yeah but I don't have a PC, I have a Mac. So that's what Sally says, and I glance over and I see that there is this thing about technology, I'm not pitching by the way or maybe I am pitching but I am going through my training, and then I come back and I say hey, you know one of the things that's so important about how you're setting up your Facebook ads and using this particular software tool is that it's software as a service meaning it's on the web, that means it doesn't matter what web browser I'm using, it doesn't matter if I'm using a Mac or PC, guess what?

All I do is use my web browsers and I go two clicks and I type in a couple of words and it doesn't matter that I'm on a Mac or on a PC

. And by doing that even though it's only one person, Sally is like he just read my mind, I was just thinking about that. And here's what happens too is that Sally doesn't have any idea whatsoever that you answered her objection, you just gave the answer to her, you know what that does?

You're not answering her logically Rich, because when there is an objection out there and you overtly put the objection out there it's explicit, it's overt and it's explicit, the other person on the other side knows that you're answering the objection for the sake of selling them whereas if you fold it nicely into the presentation, smooth as silk, because it's valuable, it's valuable that you can use a Mac or a PC, it's valuable, you've just shared that, you answered the objection, the resistance is extremely low, you're doing mindreading, and rather than being rational and rather than being logical do you know what happens?

It's emotional Rich and do you sell on emotion or do you sell on logic? You sell on emotion, so this is why it's a secret within a secret within a secret. I said it's operations, I then said look you handle the objection as close to real time as you can, that's a trick in of itself.

The secret within that secret is you smoothly weave it in, you never bring the objection up, you've solved the objection and now it's just emotionally…. The person actually feels relief, they feel good about you, about your awareness, about your third eye, about your chakras, who knows, they feel it.

Rich: All of that stuff I totally agree. John I want to thank you for taking this time with us, it was just great and informative, you've given us a bunch of great tips. If someone wanted to get a hold of you and perhaps have you host a webinar or maybe you could help them, got an email address where people can say hey?

John: Absolutely. The best email and this is my personal email address because I know Rich only brings the best, the brightest, the most highly qualified folks who has sort of made it through the gauntlet, you want to utilize this email address so write this one down, it's going to be John.rhodes@gmail.com, and if you want to see what I am doing webinar wise head over to Facebook and do a search for Juggernaut IQ and I'm constantly dropping in great new information, I talk about my webinars, I talk about other people, I do Facebook live over on juggernaut IQ, so it's a great way to socially connect with me as well.

Rich: Awesome. Juggernaut IQ that's how you can get to John's Facebook page, john.rhodes@gmail.com. John it's been an absolute privilege and a pleasure to have you on here, certainly you went beyond expectations and I can't thank you enough and I'm sure the people who are watching or listening or reading can't thank you enough as well, so thank you.

John: My pleasure. Thanks so much for having me on Rich, I really appreciate it. thank you.

Rich: Thank you and you're a gentleman *** among other things. That's going to wrap it up for our 50k webinar blueprint for today, whether you're reading it, listening to it, watching it or just taking that information, absorb the information, they say knowledge is power and you've got a lot of knowledge today but more importantly it's the use of that knowledge that's the power, so go ahead and use what you learned. On behalf of myself and my family I want to thank everybody for joining us on 50k webinar blueprint, we'll see you another time once again on 50k webinar blueprint. So long everybody.

CONCLUSION:

Well there you have it. I am in awe and I have learned so much by conducting these interviews with these amazing Internet marketers.

The tips and tricks that I learned in this book I've implemented in my product, 50 K webinar blueprint, which you can purchase on JVs it will or you can get on my website, www.Richwilens.comh

If you would like to be an affiliate for this book, program, or www.richwilens.com , please contact me on my website. I am available for webinars, in fact I call it a webinar on webinars, and I promise you and your list will greatly benefit.

Thanks for reading this book.

ABOUT THE AUTHOR:

Rich Wilens has hosted over 400 different webinars for JVZoo's sister company Webnarswaps. His latest projects include two book's **Everything Webinars: a complete guide to creating the perfect sales converting webinar or production presentation** and **10X your webinar** to be released March 2016.

Rich's sales experience begins in 1976 working and learning from the great sales trainer Tom Hopkins. Rich went on to gain his experience how people think and how to close the sale for over 40 years in various niches closing sales..

Selling everything and closing thousands of sales, Rich has taken his experience and converted his mastery of closing the sale and designed his latest program specifically for Webinars and product presentations

Rich has a style that closes more sales. His Book: Objection Overruled was called the most stolen book in Car Dealerships. Rich can close the sale.

Now, he brings his experience to you after working with JVZoo and Webinarswaps from the beginning, Rich takes your webinar and product presentation to the next level.

Rich Wilens is available for speaking events, corporate and comedy events,

Joint Venture with me, radio and television interviews and Internet Marketing workshops.

You can contact Rich at:

www.richwilens.com

Skype: rich.wilens

Facebook: https://www.facebook.com/rich.wilens

Email: richwilens1@yahoo.com,

Telephone: 228-238-7573

Made in the USA
Charleston, SC
16 September 2016